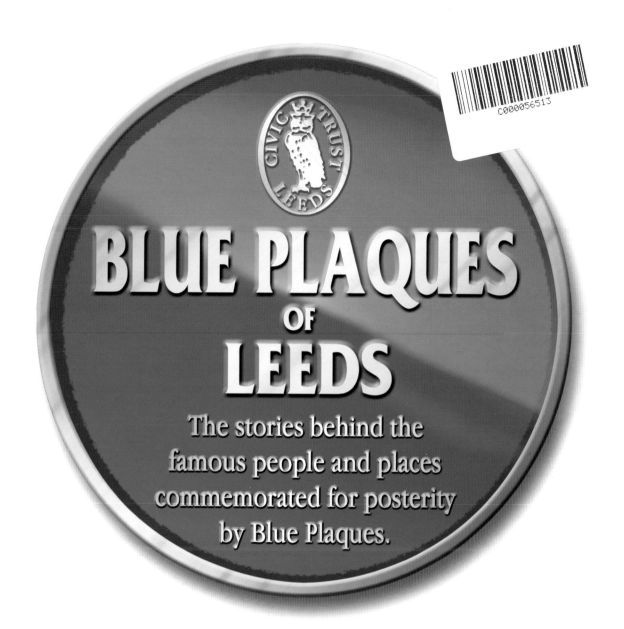

BLUE PLAQUES
OF
LEEDS

The stories behind the
famous people and places
commemorated for posterity
by Blue Plaques.

Peter Dyson and Kevin Grady

Published by Leeds Civic Trust 2001

Design and Artwork by Oyster, Leeds

Printed By Hawthornes, Nottingham

ISBN 0 905671228

CONTENTS

PREFACE

Leeds Civic Trust established the Blue Plaques Scheme to honour some of the great people and some of the important buildings that have shaped our city.

Neville Rowell and Tony Moyes originally proposed a plaques scheme for Leeds. They maintained their enthusiasm for this project and after Trust Council meetings in January and May 1986 it was agreed to start.

The first unveiling was of the Burley Bar Stone Plaque, by the entrance of the Leeds and Holbeck Building Society on 27th November 1987. At 31st March 2001 sixty-six plaques have been unveiled drawing attention to many aspects of life in Leeds.

A number of people have been involved in the scheme, but above all we must praise Valerie Ives for her contribution to its continuing success. Throughout the fourteen years of the Plaques Scheme, Valerie has carried the administrative burden of choosing the sites, finding sponsors, agreeing texts, placing orders for manufacture and arranging the unveiling ceremonies.

Amongst the benefits of the scheme have been the entertaining and informative short talks about the subject of the plaques given at their unveiling. These have usually been given by Dr. Kevin Grady, sometimes by Steven Burt, and occasionally by other members of the Trust.

This book is intended to give a wider knowledge of the subjects commemorated by the plaques. It is largely based on the talks given at the unveiling of each plaque, and from reading many of the books about the history of different aspects of life in Leeds. The authors are grateful to all the people who have freely contributed their help and advice in producing this book.

It will perhaps stimulate thoughts about other buildings or personalities who should be commemorated in this way as the Blue Plaques Scheme is continuing beyond the sixty-six included in this book.

EARLY HISTORY

The visitor today to the great industrial and commercial city of Leeds can scarcely conceive that once upon a time it was an inconsequential medieval agricultural settlement but so it was. At the time of the Domesday Book in 1086 Leeds was a small manor on the north bank of the River Aire. With the present-day area of the City Centre at its core, to the east the manor comprised Knostrop, Richmond Hill, Burmantofts and Harehills. Directly north it took in Quarry Hill, Sheepscar and Chapeltown. To the west and north-west, it encompassed Buslingthorpe and Woodhouse Ridge (with Meanwood Beck as its northern boundary) and swept down the Hyde Park Road side of Woodhouse Moor to the River Aire on Kirkstall Road, just next to the Yorkshire Television Studios.

The core of the medieval village remained Kirkgate and the Parish Church until 1207 when the Lord of the Manor, Maurice Paynel, in a bid to make some money, created the long broad market place, which today we know as Briggate, as the heart of his new manorial borough. Over the coming centuries Briggate did become the central street of Leeds and the crafts and trades pursued by the medieval burgesses, and the growing importance of the market, enabled the village at the heart of an agricultural manor to become a thriving market town.

The key to the growth of the town of Leeds was the woollen cloth industry. During the fourteenth century two water-powered fulling mills were built on the river close to Leeds Bridge and tenterframes were erected on the banks of the river. In 1534 John Leland noted that the town 'standith most by clothing'. Cloth-making flourished in Leeds in the late sixteenth and early seventeenth centuries to such an extent that a prosperous group of cloth merchants was established which started to gain a firm grip on the market for cloth, made not only by the handicraft clothiers of Leeds, but also those in a considerable surrounding area. There was great wealth to be made.

Foremost amongst the Leeds merchants was John Harrison who was the major driving force behind the town gaining its borough charter in 1626. One of his contemporaries was the merchant John Thoresby. It is our good fortune that his son Ralph Thoresby proved to have little aptitude for cloth trading and instead devoted much of his life to antiquarian pursuits. Ralph's diaries and letters and his great book on the history and topography of Leeds provide invaluable information about the history of seventeenth and early eighteenth century Leeds.

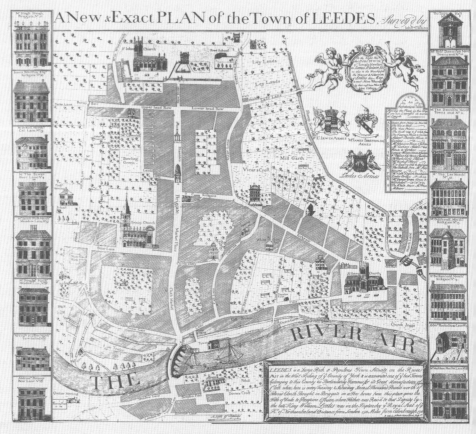

COSSINS' PLAN OF LEEDS 1726

Leeds Manor House

The medieval manor house stood here on 'Castle Hill'. Its deep moat looped between the river and Boar Lane. Richard Wilson lavishly rebuilt it in 1765 and in 1823 it became Henry Scarbrough's hotel. The present-day pub is a surviving extension.

'Leeds Castle' or fortified manor house was built by the de Lacy family of Pontefract at the end of the eleventh century on the present-day site of the Scarbrough public house in Bishopgate Street. As the manor was held by absentee landlords the castle was probably used infrequently, and had been demolished by the fourteenth century. In 1341 a survey of the manor recorded that the manor house had gone but that its site was still moated and included an enclosed courtyard and another enclosure in which some farm buildings had been built. Ralph Thoresby suggested that the stone from the manor house was used to build the medieval bridge.

A new manor house was built here in the sixteenth century and it was this building which was remodelled by Richard Wilson, the principal legal officer of Leeds Corporation, and is shown on Cossins' Plan of 1726. His descendant, also Richard Wilson, rebuilt it as an imposing mansion house with lovely gardens running down to the river in 1765. In 1815 the adjacent surviving wing of the seventeenth century manor house was acquired by Henry Scarbrough for the King's Arms public house.

A notice was placed in the Leeds newspaper in June 1815, headed 'King's Arms, Mill-Hill, Leeds. H. Scarbrough begs leave to inform the inhabitants of Leeds and its vicinity, that he has opened the above inn, and trusts, from his attention to the comfort of his guests, to merit their support. In consequence of the unfinished state of the upper part of the house, H.S. is sorry he is not at present provided with beds, but will be in the course of a fortnight. N.B. Very superior stabling.'

Opening an unfinished hotel is not just a present day phenomenon!

In 1823 Scarbrough also acquired the 1765 manor house and turned it into Scarbrough's Hotel. A later report about an evening spent by a small group of local worthy gentlemen says that Scarbrough's Hotel was the best in Leeds by far. The diners had a very good meal, there was salmon and soles; then boiled fowls and ham, roast beef, roast ducks and pastry. They had some excellent wine, Bucellas, Moselle, Sherry, Port and Claret. Having ordered dinner for six o'clock the diners set off for home at one in the morning. They admitted to taking rather too much wine.

In 1857 the Prince of Wales - later King Edward VII - and his entourage were accommodated at Scarbrough's on their way to Harewood House. Charles Dickens stayed at Scarbrough's in September 1858, and he wrote a letter to his sister from here telling her of the grand celebrations for Queen Victoria opening the Town Hall.

The inn was one of Leeds outstanding singing rooms in Victorian days - not so grand as the music halls of which the City Varieties Music Hall is a surviving example.

The Scarbrough Hotel was demolished in the 1930s, but the Scarbrough Taps (originally the King's Arms and the wing of the seventeenth century manor house) is still a place of resort for city drinkers today.

The Leeds Manor House Plaque was sponsored by Joshua Tetley & Sons Ltd and was unveiled by Professor Maurice Beresford, the eminent Leeds historian, on 26th September 1989. It is at the Scarbrough Hotel, Bishopgate Street, Leeds 1.

The Bar Stones

BURLEY BAR STONE

This stone, now housed inside the main entrance of Leeds & Holbeck Building Society, marked the medieval boundary between the manorial borough, or town, of Leeds and Leeds Main Riding, the surrounding agricultural land. First recorded 1725.

In the Middle Ages the boundaries of the built-up area of the town of Leeds were marked by bars. Leeds was not a heavily defended city like York, and so did not have large stone fortified entrances similar to Bootham Bar and Micklegate Bar. John Cossins' Plan of Leeds 1726 indicates that some, if not all, the Leeds bars were wooden gates, to keep out cattle and to delay unwanted visitors.

Originally, there were six town bars. Moving in a clockwise direction they were: **A.** Burley Bar on the Headrow, by Albion Street; **B.** Woodhouse Bar at the bottom of Woodhouse Lane, in Dortmund Square; **C.** North Bar on Vicar Lane, between Lady Lane and Templar Street; **D.** East Bar, or York Bar, at the end of Kirkgate by the Parish Church; **E.** South Bar on the south side of Leeds Bridge; **F.** West Bar towards the City Square end of Boar Lane.

By the eighteenth century the bars had ceased to be of physical significance, but they marked important administrative boundaries. Their position was thereafter marked by Bar Stones. The Burley Bar Stone and the East Bar Stone can still be seen, the North Bar Stone is also still in place, but is hidden behind a shop facade.

In 1755 the Leeds Improvement Act empowered a commission consisting of fourteen principal inhabitants living within the town bars, nominated by the ratepayers, plus the Mayor, Recorder and Justices of the Peace for the borough, to provide street lighting and paving for the streets within the bars and to ensure that the town was properly cleansed. Under the Act residents within the town bars were required to 'cease throwing ashes, rubbish, dust, timber, dirt, dung, filth, tubs or other annoyances into the streets'. Occupants of houses fronting the street were obliged to 'sweep and clean the street in front of their property between one and three o'clock every Saturday afternoon'.

It is interesting to note that the boundaries denoted by the bars in the early eighteenth century conform very closely to the boundaries of the Leeds city centre shopping area today. The siting of the West Bar and Burley Bar are readily explained because they marked the boundary between the town and the manorial park. Even when the trees had been cut down, the park area remained open fields well into the eighteenth century until the development of the Park Estate began. Park Row was the first of the streets to be built. The river to

the south created a very natural boundary. Cossins' Plan shows that beyond the Parish Church to the east, and St. John's Church and the Grammar School to the north there were open fields.

The rapid growth of the town after 1755 made it necessary to extend street lighting, paving and the authority of the street cleaning by-laws beyond the bars. The 1790 Improvement Act, which included provisions to do with water supply, extended the commissioners' jurisdiction to 'areas within one thousand yards of the town bars'.

EAST BAR

This ancient stone marked the eastern boundary of the medieval town of Leeds.

THE WEST BAR

The bar stone marking the western boundary of the built - up area of the medieval town of Leeds stood here. Scarcely a single building lay in the old manorial park to the west of this point before 1758.

The Burley Bar Stone Plaque was the first blue plaque to be unveiled by the Leeds Civic Trust. It was sponsored by Leeds & Holbeck Building Society and unveiled by Lord Marshall of Leeds, President of Leeds Civic Trust and former leader of Leeds City Council, on 27th November 1987. It is by the entrance of the Leeds & Holbeck Building Society, The Headrow, Leeds 1.

The East Bar Plaque was sponsored by Professor N. R. Rowell, Vice President of Leeds Civic Trust, and was also unveiled by him on 23rd May 1995. It is at the Parish Church, Kirkgate, Leeds 2.

The West Bar Plaque was sponsored by Bond Street Shopping Centre Merchants' Association, and unveiled by Councillor J. L. Carter, Lord Mayor of Leeds on 19th September 1989. It is at the Bond Street Centre, Boar Lane, Leeds 1.

THE WEST BAR

The bar stone marking the western boundary of the built-up area of the medieval town of Leeds stood here. Scarcely a single building lay in the old manorial park to the west of this point before 1758.

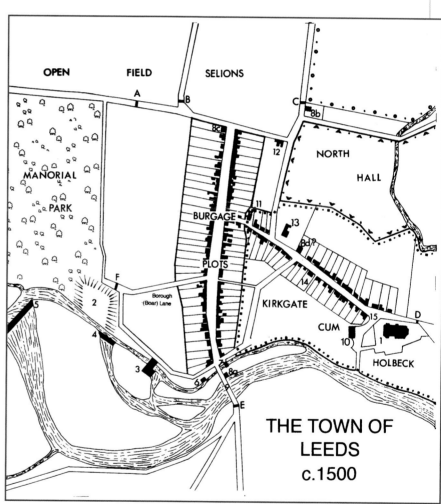

THE TOWN OF LEEDS c.1500

LEEDS IN THE LATE MEDIEVAL PERIOD.

KEY:

1. St. Peter's — the parish church
2. Castelhyll — site of the former fortified manor house
3. Manorial Corn Mill
4. Bondman Dam
5. High Dam
6. Fulling mill
7. Fulling mill
8. Chantry Chapels:
a. St. Mary's on the Bridge
b. Lady Chapel
c. Sir William Eures' Chapel
d. Thomas Clarell's Chapel
9. Leeds Bridge
10. Tithe Barn
11. Manorial Oven with Hall of Pleas above
12. Rockley Hall
13. The Vicarage
14. The Hospitium.
15. Manor house of Kirkgate-cum-Holbeck

The Bars — the boundaries of the medieval town
A. Burley Bar.
B. Woodhouse Bar.
C. North Bar.
D. East or York Bar.
E. South Bar.
F. West Bar.

John Harrison

1579 - 1656

St. John's, one of England's most remarkable churches, was built by this celebrated benefactor in 1634. A cloth merchant and co-founder of Leeds Corporation, he further endowed the town with almshouses, a new grammar school and a market cross.

John Harrison's father, also called John Harrison, was a woollen merchant from a Gipton family. His mother, Elizabeth Marton, was from a family of Holbeck clothiers. He was the only son, but had two sisters, Edith and Grace. John Harrison's father died in 1601, his mother in 1602. He married Elizabeth Foxcroft of Headingley in 1603 and shortly afterwards built a brick house at the east end of Boar Lane, described by Thoresby as 'a good old fashioned house with a quadrangular court in the midst....and has one thing very peculiar in it, viz, holes and passages cut in the doors and wainscots for the free passage of cats for which animals he seems to have had as great an affection as another famous benefactor had viz - Sir Richard Whittington.' Harrison became the wealthiest woollen merchant in Leeds and extremely influential in local affairs.

As a result of John Metcalfe, the manorial bailiff of Leeds, being found guilty of embezzling funds intended for the poor, the Pious Uses Committee was set up in 1619 to administer local charities. John Harrison was one of the leading townsmen appointed to this committee.

With the help of Sir John Savile of Howley Hall, Leeds was granted the Borough Charter of 1626, giving Leeds its first town council. The first alderman was Sir John Savile, but Harrison acted as his deputy, and became alderman in his own right in 1634. As a member of the corporation and one of the lords of the manor he was a member of the merchant elite who dominated the affairs of Leeds until the Civil War (1642 - 1648).

Harrison followed his father's example of buying property, and used the rents and profits to finance his acts of charity. Shortly after his marriage he bought the North Hall and Rockley Hall estates. Two rooms in Rockley Hall were used as storerooms for food and clothing for the poor. In 1619 he endowed a Market Cross in Briggate. In 1624 John Harrison provided land and a new building for the Grammar School - on the site of the present Grand Theatre.

In 1631, the year in which his wife died, John Harrison built St. John's Church, which was consecrated on 21st September 1634, and the twenty almshouses to the west of the church which housed 'forty indigent persons of good conversation and formerly industrious.'

Having no heirs he made charitable benefactions which still benefit the people of Leeds today, most notably the almshouses by Woodhouse Moor.

The John Harrison Plaque was sponsored by Professor N. R. Rowell, Vice President of Leeds Civic Trust, and unveiled by him on 29th August 1991. It is on St. John's Churchyard Wall, New Briggate, Leeds 1.

Ralph Thoresby, F R S

1658 - 1725

The historian of Leeds had his home and museum here.

Ralph Thoresby was born at the house that stood at 15 Kirkgate on 16th August 1658. His father, John Thoresby, was a Leeds merchant and had served as an officer in the Parliamentary army under Fairfax. Both father and son were deeply religious and shared a common interest in antiquity and collecting.

Ralph is reputed to have attended Leeds Grammar School and acquired a knowledge of Latin and Greek. In 1677 he stayed with relatives in London to prepare for a career in business. He spent eight months abroad during the following year learning Dutch and French, and completing his business training.

When his father died in 1679 Ralph had to assume full responsibility for the business. In 1685 he married Ann Sykes, a daughter of Richard Sykes of Ledsham, one of the Lords of the Manor of Leeds.

Ralph began keeping a diary in September 1677 and kept it going - with some gaps - to 1724. The diary was published together with a volume of correspondence in the 1830s. It is an indispensable source for the study of late seventeenth and early eighteenth century Leeds.

It was historical research, genealogy and curiosities which were Thoresby's great interests. At his house in Kirkgate, Leeds had its first recorded museum. John Thoresby had purchased a fine collection of coins and medals from the Fairfax family, and Ralph had continued to collect a wide range of manuscripts, geological specimens, relics and curiosities. He also received many gifts of natural history objects from all over the world. From about 1692 the museum attracted the attention of local people and visitors to Leeds. Unfortunately the museum did not survive his death. He bequeathed the collection to his son, the Reverend Ralph Thoresby, Rector of Stoke Newington, on whose death the collection was auctioned and dispersed.

Ralph Thoresby was elected a Fellow of the Royal Academy in 1697 and made many contributions to the society's Transactions.

In 1715 Thoresby published the first part of a topography and history of Leeds, entitled *Ducatus Leodiensis*. This provides a street by street description of early Georgian Leeds, and includes two plans and two prospects of the town.

The Ralph Thoresby Plaque was sponsored by the Thoresby Society and unveiled by Mr. Arthur Elton, President of the Thoresby Society, on 6th October 1992. It is at 15, Kirkgate, Leeds 2.

THE GEORGIAN MARKET TOWN

Despite the ravages of the Civil War and the plague of 1645, the population of the town had increased to 6,000 by 1700. A century of growing prosperity saw its population leap to over 16,000 by 1770 and astonishingly almost double over the next thirty years. Rising prosperity financed the replacement of many half-timbered merchant houses with the fashionable brick town houses of the kind shown on John Cossins' Plan of 1726. Meanwhile, since the physical boundaries of the built-up area hardly grew at all, the town became crowded with new houses constructed in the yards, orchards and gardens bordering the main streets. Warehouses, cloth finishing shops, inns and shops too, sprang up behind the principal frontages.

The creation of the Aire and Calder Navigation in 1699-1700 established Leeds as a major inland port. This, and the building of several large cloth halls which superseded the Briggate cloth market, enabled the thriving Leeds merchant community to gain almost complete dominance of the West Riding woollen cloth industry. The first White Cloth Hall, built in Kirkgate in 1710-11, and still surviving today, is shown above. By 1770 Leeds merchants handled over one-third of all woollen cloth exported from England, remarkably giving them a one-sixth share of the entire domestically produced exports of the country.

Wealth generated by the cloth trade and cloth manufacture in Leeds and its district created a prosperity which few other towns in England exceeded. The market generated by the thousands of clothiers who poured into Leeds on market days and its rapidly growing population enabled Leeds to become a centre for entertainment and wholesale distribution, for books and newspapers, wallpaper, chinaware, bricks, tailoring, and the best wigs, medical treatment, legal services, inns and coach travel.

By the end of the century, in addition to these trades and those associated with cloth making, Leeds could boast salters, chandlers, braziers, coachmakers, white and blacksmiths, jewellers, clockmakers, tailors, shoemakers, wine merchants, printers, undertakers, builders, teachers, bankers, clergymen, ropers, glovers, timber merchants, insurance agents and many other trades and professions.

In short, during the eighteenth century it became one of the busiest and most vibrant market towns in England. The great wealth generated was used in part to promote the town's social facilities. By the 1790s Leeds had assembly rooms, a theatre, concert hall, music hall, subscription library as well as new churches and chapels.

White Cloth Hall

Built between 1775 and 1776, this superbly restored gateway belonged to the magnificent quadrangular market hall which underpinned the prosperity of Georgian Leeds. Merchants and 1300 West Riding clothiers met here on Tuesdays and Saturdays to trade in undyed 'white' woollen cloth.

This building was the third of a series of White Cloth Halls built in Leeds. The first White Cloth Hall on Kirkgate was opened in 1711, the second in Meadow Lane in 1755, and the third here in The Calls in 1776. Each hall superseded its predecessor as larger accommodation was required to match the rapid growth of the cloth trade. The third hall had a quadrangle 99 yards by 70 yards. The comfort of the covered accommodation, which allowed the pattern of the street market to be replicated away from the elements, enabled the Leeds merchants to fight off initially strong competition from the Wakefield cloth merchants for dominance in the West Riding cloth industry.

The bulk of the undyed woollen cloth made by the clothiers of the West Riding during the seventeenth and eighteenth centuries was brought here on pack horses on Tuesdays and Saturdays. They were sure of a ready sale in Leeds because of its efficient, enterprising and highly successful cloth merchant community. In 1765 between four and five thousand clothiers attended the Leeds cloth halls each week. In the 1770s there were more than 70 firms of cloth merchants in the town. One third of all woollen cloth exported from England was handled by Leeds merchants, amounting to some £1,500,000 a year at a time when a worker's cottage cost about £40 to £50.

Not all the buying and selling of cloth was carried out in the cloth halls. The practice of buying cloth by direct order from the clothier was well established by the mid-eighteenth century, but the greater part of the business was conducted in the cloth halls into the nineteenth century. The Industrial Revolution, and particularly the enterprise of Benjamin Gott in setting up the world's first large woollen mill at Park Mills, Bean Ing, Leeds, begun in 1792, started the decline in their importance. This is reflected in the reduction in the price of stands in the White Cloth Hall from between £6 and £8 in 1800 to no more than £1 in 1822, and a sharp fall in the number of independent clothiers attending the hall. This hall was closed in 1866 by the companies building the new railway station and viaduct. They replaced it with a new White Cloth Hall on the site of the old Infirmary Gardens, King Street.

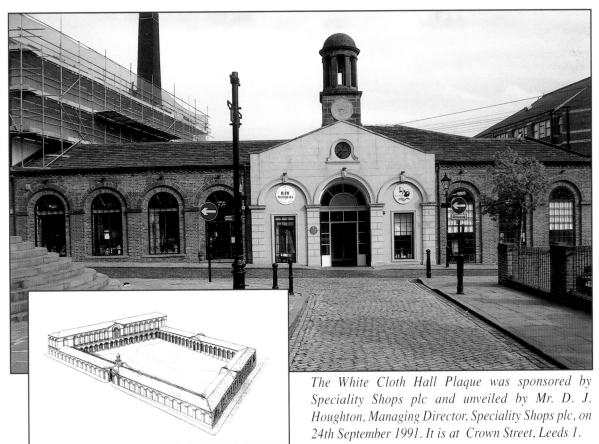

The White Cloth Hall Plaque was sponsored by Speciality Shops plc and unveiled by Mr. D. J. Houghton, Managing Director, Speciality Shops plc, on 24th September 1991. It is at Crown Street, Leeds 1.

Coloured Cloth Hall

Leeds' most splendid Georgian cloth hall, built in 1758, stood on this site. Projecting to the centre of City Square, its massive quadrangular structure housed 1770 stalls for clothiers selling dyed woollen cloth at the Tuesday and Saturday markets.

During the seventeenth century the famous woollen cloth market was held in Briggate but due to competition from other towns and the need for improved facilities the merchants and clothiers decided to bring the cloth market under cover. When in 1710 the cloth hall was erected in Kirkgate for the sale of white cloth (undyed cloth) by sample this left a substantial part of the market for white cloth and the whole of the market for dyed cloth still in Briggate. When the second White Cloth Hall was erected in Meadow Lane in 1755, however, only coloured clothiers remained in Briggate. As a major part of the cloth trade they naturally demanded a large and comfortable hall of their own. In 1758 the Coloured Cloth Hall was erected at the junction of Park Row and Infirmary Street. The coloured clothiers making cloth with handcraft equipment in their homes, specialised in the production of cloth whose wool was dyed before it was woven - hence 'coloured cloth'. In later years they also produced cloth using a variation of woollen and worsted fibres in the warp and weft, consequently the Coloured Cloth Hall was sometimes referred to as the Mixed Cloth Hall.

The Coloured Cloth Hall was very impressive, being the largest building in Georgian Leeds. It accommodated 1700 clothiers on market days who occupied small stalls in the alleys and wings of the building. The hall measured 127 yards by 66 yards.

THE COLOURED CLOTH HALL

With the development of the factory system, trade drained away from the Coloured Cloth Hall as it had done from the White Cloth Hall, as merchants dealt directly with manufacturers. By the 1830s it was in severe decline, but remained open until 1889. In 1890 it was demolished for the erection of the Post Office building in City Square.

The Coloured Cloth Hall Plaque was sponsored by Hepworth & Chadwick, Solicitors and unveiled by Mr. D. F. L. Sykes, Senior Partner, Hepworth & Chadwick, on 16th May 1991. It is at Cloth Hall Court, Infirmary Street, Leeds

THE COLOURED CLOTH HALL (1758)

Kirkgate Market

In 1826 the Leeds vicarage and croft were purchased to create a fruit , vegetable and cattle market. An elegant Crystal Palace-style covered market was erected in 1857, followed in 1904 by today's magnificent market hall designed by Leeming and Leeming.

For over six hundred years Leeds market was centred on Briggate. Briggate was designed to be a large market place, and medieval records detailing disputes over the siting of market stalls, problems over false measures and court actions for non-payment of market tolls give a flavour of the rough and tumble and bustle of this important regional market.

In the seventeenth century Briggate was particularly famous as the site of the nationally important woollen cloth market. During the eighteenth century the cloth market was held on Tuesdays and Saturdays. Describing Briggate in 1715, Ralph Thoresby (see page 9) explained how, when the cloth market was finished and the clothiers' trestle tables were removed, the street was filled with sellers of all descriptions: 'the market people of other professions, such as Country Linen Drapers, Shoo-makers, Hard-waremen, and the sellers of Wood Vessels, Wicker Baskets, Wanded Chairs, Flakes (fences) etc.; the fruit sellers both wholesale and retail; the farmers selling dairy cattle; the fish traders; the butchers in the Shambles behind the Moothall; the egg, butter and poultry sellers; and the corn traders.'

Briggate was also the main north-south route through Leeds. Despite the removal of the cloth market to the Coloured and White Cloth Halls, the volume of trade in other goods became so great that by the 1820s the congestion on market days demanded urgent action. Kirkgate Market began its life in 1826 when the Leeds Improvement Commissioners bought the Leeds Vicarage and its field and moved in to it the Briggate fruit and vegetable market and the Vicar Lane cattle market. In 1857 the first Kirkgate Market Hall was built on the site. It was an amazing glass and cast iron building designed with the advice of Sir Joseph Paxton, the designer of the Crystal Palace.

In 1875 extensive rows of shops were added to the back of the market hall. These survive today as Butchers' Row, Game Row and the adjacent rows where fruit and vegetables and fish are sold (now the oldest part of the market). A few years later further wholesale accommodation and a fish market were added at the lower end of the market. It was these parts which were burned down in the disastrous fire in 1975 which threatened the future of the market.

In 1904 the Victorian market hall was replaced by the splendid Leeds City Market Hall designed by Leeming and Leeming. Today this is one of the finest market halls in the country.

The Kirkgate Market Millennium Blue Plaque was sponsored by Richard Wainwright, formerly Liberal MP for the Colne Valley, and was unveiled by him on 14th December 2000. It is at the Vicar Lane end of Butchers' Row in Kirkgate Market, Leeds 2.

PARK MILLS, BEAN ING, BEGUN BY BENJAMIN GOTT IN 1792 - THE WORLD'S FIRST WOOLLEN MILL

INVENTION & INDUSTRY

Between 1790 and 1840 the character and landscape of Leeds was transformed by the arrival of the factory age. It was an age both exciting and traumatic. Vast fortunes were made and yet many livelihoods were ruined as handicraft production slowly but surely became outmoded or production moved into mills.

In the 1790s Benjamin Gott created the world's first woollen mill at Bean Ing, while in Holbeck John Marshall pioneered the Leeds flax-spinning industry. Both were millionaires by the late 1820s and with workforces of over 1000 were amongst the largest employers in England. In Holbeck too, Matthew Murray, a former employee of Marshall's, founded the Leeds engineering industry making textile machinery and steam engines rivalling those of Boulton and Watt. From the early nineteenth century mill chimneys began to dominate the Leeds skyline.

While the cloth-making industry remained strong throughout the Victorian era, its dominance was challenged by the arrival or rapid expansion of many other industries. The fast expanding engineering industry was complemented by astonishing growth in brewing, food-processing, tanning, shoe-making, pottery manufacture, the production of ready-made clothing, printing, and chemicals. Large-scale factories, though, were the exception rather than the rule. Impressive as they were, often it was the sheer diversity of Leeds industry that amazed visitors. Leeds' reputation as 'the city of a thousand trades' was well earned.

The city attracted and encouraged men with entrepreneurial flair, many of whom became household names and leading lights in the life of Leeds. Prime examples were Joshua Tetley in brewing, John Barran in ready-made clothing, Thomas Harding producing textile manufacturing equipment at Tower Works, William Potts with his famous clocks and, in the twentieth century, Montague Burton with his tailoring empire. Others' exertions achieved them fame only in later years. Two such talents were Joseph Aspdin, who invented Portland cement in a Briggate yard in the 1820s, and Louis Le Prince, the pioneer of cinematography.

The spirit of the Victorian age was that with energy and imagination any one could get on in life. The great propagandist of this philosophy was Samuel Smiles with his doctrine of 'Self-help'. He too played a significant part in the life of Victorian Leeds.

Temple Mill

The magnificent but highly functional flax-spinning mill was erected by John Marshall, founder of the Leeds Flax Industry, between 1838 and 1840. Joseph Bonomi modelled it and this office building (added in 1843) on the Egyptian temple at Edfu.

The architectural style of Temple Mill makes it the most remarkable industrial building in Leeds. It is an amazing experience to walk down a small side street in an industrial area and to be confronted by an Egyptian temple.

In 1787 at the age of 22, John Marshall, a Briggate linen draper, set up a water-powered flax-spinning mill at Scotland Mill on the Meanwood Beck near Adel. In 1791 he moved into Leeds where he erected a new mill in Water Lane, Holbeck, which was convenient for the Leeds and Liverpool Canal, coal supply from Middleton Colliery, water power from the Hol Beck and for recruiting a large work-force. He soon installed a Boulton & Watt steam engine to power the flax-spinning machinery.

The rapid growth of the business necessitated further new buildings, and in the late 1830s the revolutionary decision was taken not to build a multi-storey factory, but instead to erect a vast single-storey building covering almost two acres.

It was roofed by brick arches supported by cast-iron columns (which also acted as rainwater pipes), and the work space gained natural light from sixty-five glass domes. To prevent rainwater penetrating the flat roof, the brick vaults were covered on the outside by roof plaster, then by a mixture of coal tar and lime to form a waterproof barrier. Surface water drained down the inside of the cast-iron columns. To insulate the delicate waterproof membrane it was covered with an eight inch layer of earth, sown with grass to hold it in place.

The need to keep this grass short gives credence to popular tradition in Leeds that sheep grazed on the factory roof. Over one thousand people were working in this mill. Its design was so remarkable that Benjamin Disraeli described it in his novel, *Sybil*.

The architect Joseph Bonomi had spent eight years in Egypt studying ancient architecture and was the acknowledged expert on the temples at Karnak, Edfu and Philae. The mill's cast iron columns have palm capitals; outside, the millstone grit ashlar walls contain large cast iron window frames interspersed by half columns with papyrus capitals.

Bonomi was able to lavish even more detailed antiquarian knowledge on the design of the office building, added in 1843. The furniture was of Egyptian design and the building had a screen facade carefully copied from the portico of the Temple of Horus at Edfu.

The Temple Mill Plaque was sponsored by Kay & Company Ltd and unveiled by Mr. Bruce Taylor on 14th February 1989. It is at Marshall Street, Leeds 11.

Bank Mills

This magnificent waterside flax mill and its twin block just upstream were designed by architect John Clark and built in 1831-2 for Messrs Hives and Atkinson, former partners of John Marshall the famous Leeds flax spinner.

Bank Mills is a monument to the industrial history of Leeds. It is also a monument to the thousands of Irish immigrants who lived in the slums of the Bank area of Leeds, and whose womenfolk found employment as mill girls in Bank Mills. While the flax industry brought great prosperity to Leeds, and provided these immigrants with a livelihood, working conditions in the industry were appalling. The factory became infamous in the 1830s when the working conditions of its employees were highlighted in reports to Parliament. Due to the damp, humid and incredibly dusty atmosphere of the mills, workers rapidly developed respiratory disorders. At the same time there were many serious injuries to workers by inadequately guarded machinery.

In the 1790s John Marshall founded the flax-spinning industry in Leeds. Two of his mills, including the Egyptian style Temple Mill survive in Holbeck. Less well known, but also of huge significance is Bank Mills built by Messrs Hives and Atkinson.

In 1804 Marshall took John Hives, his employee, into partnership and in 1810 John Atkinson, his chief clerk, was also made a partner.

In 1823, when Marshall felt that Hives and Atkinson had outlived their usefulness, he terminated the partnership. They, however, were determined to stay in the flax business and their eyes turned to Bank Mills.

In 1791 Markland Cookson and Fawcett had built a cotton-spinning mill beside the River Aire at the Bank. Its designer was John Sutcliffe of Halifax who had just completed the new Armley Mills for Thomas Lloyd. Originally it was powered by a fourteen foot water wheel on Timble Beck, but this was replaced in 1792 by a 30 h.p. beam engine by Boulton & Watt. The mill continued to spin cotton up to 1797, and wool for their carpet and worsted factories, until about 1819. In 1824 Hives and Atkinson acquired the mill and installed flax-spinning equipment but the property was soon destroyed by a fire. New mills of fireproof construction were erected to the design of John Clark of Edinburgh in 1824, 1831-32, and 1832-33 to accommodate their booming flax-spinning business.

Today Bank Mills, now known as Rose Wharf, is a majestic piece of Leeds' architectural heritage occupying a spectacular location on a bend of the River Aire. It was renovated and converted for modern office uses in 1997 by Caddick Developments. The architects were Carey Jones.

The Bank Mills Plaque was sponsored by Caddick Developments and by Carey Jones, Architects. It was unveiled by Mr. Gordon Carey RIBA, Chairman of Carey Jones, Architects, on 12th March 1999. It is at Rose Wharf, East Street, Leeds 9.

St. Paul's House

This building was originally a warehouse and cloth-cutting works designed by architect Thomas Ambler and built in 1878 for John Barran, the founder of the mass-production, ready-made clothing industry in Leeds. Barran was a Mayor of Leeds and served as its Liberal M.P. from 1876 - 1885.

News of 17th January 1879 noted: 'The site on which this building stands is situate on the south side of Park Square, and was formerly occupied by a terrace of nine good houses, which had to be taken down. The building is in the Moorish style of architecture, It is built of selected hand pressed bricks, and red and buff terra-cotta is used for the dressings. The four sides of the building are treated uniformly with the front, the north-west turret being used as a chimney to carry off the vitiated atmosphere from the gas engines, as well as from the heating apparatus.'

John Barran was born in Surrey, the son of a London gun maker. In 1841, when he was 21 years old, he came to Leeds and set up as a tailor and clothes dealer at Bridge End. By 1851 he had moved his shop to No. 2, Briggate, and had set up his own workshops where made-to-measure garments were made. He also produced ready-made garments for wholesale distribution to other clothes dealers and outfitters as well as for sale in his own shop.

In 1851 Isaac Singer invented the sewing machine, and John Barran adopted this as soon as it appeared in England. By 1856 he had some 20 to 30 sewing machines producing ready-to-wear garments in his factory in Alfred Street near his shop in Boar Lane. As the sewing machine operators improved their efficiency it became more difficult to supply them with work - a person with a pair of shears could only cut out one garment at a time. In 1858 Barran attended a furniture exhibition and watched a band saw cutting veneers. The never ending blade sliced accurately through several layers of wood. If wood, why not cloth? He soon had a Greenwood and Batley band knife cutting many layers of cloth, and the production of garments was speeded up. The mass production ready-made clothing industry was born.

In 1867 the clothing factory was moved from Alfred Street to Park Row, but soon outgrew these premises. In 1876 the architect Thomas Ambler, who had worked closely with Barran on the scheme to remodel Boar Lane, was consulted regarding designs for a model factory. This splendid building, familiar to us today, was built to Ambler's designs in 1878. *The Building*

Leeds was ideally suited for the growth of the mass-production of ready-made clothing because of its strategic position in the cloth-producing area, its large market, its engineering skills, its excellent transport facilities and its large supply of female workers used to handling cloth. Barran founded an industry.

The St. Paul's House Plaque was sponsored by Norwich Union Insurance Group and unveiled by Mr. K. E. Reynolds, Branch Manager of the Fire Society, on 3rd October 1989. It is at St. Paul's House, Park Square, Leeds 1.

Montague Burton

'The Tailor of Taste'

Making good quality, made-to-measure suits for a week's wages, Burton created a mass market. This Hudson Road headquarters, begun in 1921, was by 1925 the largest clothing factory in the world, eventually employing 10,500 people.

ARNOLD BURTON, JOHN RICHARDS, RAYMOND BURTON

The mass-production of ready-made clothes was pioneered in Leeds by John Barran in the middle of the nineteenth century. By 1881 there were 21 wholesale clothiers in Leeds. Towards the end of the century several of these firms, such as Blackburn's and Hepworth's opened chains of shops. Through these outlets they pioneered wholesale bespoke tailoring, whereby customers' measurements were taken in the shops and their suits were made back at their factories using mass-production techniques. The Leeds mass-production bespoke tailoring industry came into its own after the First World War. It experienced prodigious growth under the inspiration of its undoubted king, Montague Burton, 'The Tailor of Taste'. This giant business was founded in Sheffield in 1900 with a capital of only £100.

Burton, a Jewish refugee from Lithuania, acquired his first Leeds tailoring factory in 1909, while simultaneously pursuing plans to develop a chain of tailors shops. By 1914 Leeds had become the centre of his activities and he had specialised in the sale and manufacture of bespoke suits. Burton was a marketing genius as well as a superb organiser of production. In the years before the Second World War he was able to produce made-to-measure suits with a one week delivery, which were competitive in both price and quality with the suits made by traditional bespoke tailors and the stock garments of ready-made producers.

In 1921 he decided to transfer all his production to one new factory at Hudson Road. By 1925 it was the largest clothing factory in Europe, and became a mecca for the visits of Royalty, entertainers, politicians and sportsmen. The factory was completed in 1934 when the Princess Royal opened what was reputedly the world's largest canteen, which could accommodate 8,000 workers at one sitting, and was said to be able to serve 2,000 cups of tea in five minutes.

Burton's chain of tailors shops, with their stylish fronts and windows, grew rapidly. By 1919 he had 40 shops, rising to 224 in 1926 and to 595 by 1939. They spread from the North and Midlands to London and the South-east. By the late 1930s it was reckoned that Burton was clothing one-fifth of the male population of Britain. To meet their needs for female employees Burton had to bus in workers from within a ten mile radius of the city, and to build factories in Lancashire. In 1939 it employed 10,500 workers at Hudson Road and 6,000 in its three Lancashire factories.

Montague died in 1952. From the 1970s the rise in the importation of cheap suits and clothing from the Far East and eastern Europe and competition from better quality more fashionable clothing from western Europe hit the Leeds clothing industry. Burton concentrated on retailing, and Hudson Road ceased to manufacture in 1981, but continued to provide warehousing and office space. Retailing has continued to dominate the Burton Group, which under the name of the Arcadia Group plc, trades through its major chains of household name clothing stores including Burton, Top Shop, Top Man, Dorothy Perkins and Principles.

The Montague Burton Plaque was sponsored by the Burton family and unveiled by Mr. Arnold Burton and Mr. Raymond Burton, the twin sons of Sir Montague Burton, on 30th March 2001. It is at Hudson Road, Leeds 9.

Tower Works

Built for Harding & Son, makers of pins, cards and combs for the textile industry. Its smallest chimney (Thomas Shaw, 1864) was modelled on the Lamberti Tower in Verona, the largest (William Bakewell, 1899) on Giotto's Campanile in Florence.

Tower Works is celebrated today for its three remarkable Italianate chimneys which can be seen from many parts of the city. These were the inspiration of Colonel Thomas Walter Harding, 1843 - 1927 who was head of the firm. He was a man of great culture, having been brought up in Lille in France, and subsequently educated at Leeds Grammar School and Dresden Polytechnic. He loved Italy and chose towers in Verona, Florence and San Gimignano as models for the factory's chimneys.

Harding played a leading role in the civic life of Leeds, being Colonel of the Leeds Artillery Volunteers and Lord Mayor of Leeds in 1898/99. He made an enormous contribution to the city's cultural life. He was the prime mover behind the founding of the City Art Gallery and presented it with some of its best known paintings. He also conceived a plan for what might be done with City Square, and sent it to William Bakewell the architect, whose designs were accepted by the City Council. Harding paid for much of the statuary in the square. When the opening ceremony took place on 16th September 1903, it placed Leeds in the forefront of European civic design.

The firm of T. R. Harding started to make cast-steel pins for the gills, combs and cards used in the textile industry in 1829. When it became established on the five acre site in Globe Road, Holbeck in the 1860s it was the largest

factory of its kind in the world. Its classification for pin sizes, the Harding Gauge, became the internationally recognised standard.

In addition to making pins for the wool, flax, hemp and jute industries the company also developed a series of industrial instruments, including the 'Ideal' counter. This could count either the number of items a machine was producing, or the length of its particular product - paper, leather or other material. Their tachometer, or speed indicator, was also widely used on all types of marine and stationary engines, and on individual machines, where it enabled the number of items made in a given time to be closely monitored.

The firm became incorporated as T. R. Harding & Son Ltd in 1892. In 1895 it amalgamated with two other companies and became Harding, Rhodes & Co. After operating on this site for almost 120 years Tower Works finally closed in 1981.

The Tower Works Plaque was sponsored by Leeds Development Corporation and unveiled by Mr. Martin Eagland, Chief Executive, Leeds Development Corporation, on 25th May 1993. It is at Tower Works, Globe Road, Leeds 12.

THE ITALIANATE TOWERS FROM THE CANAL BASIN

Fletland Mills

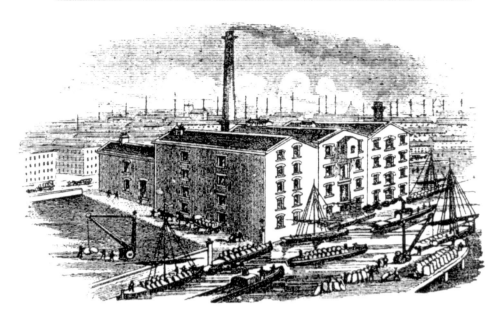

In 1887 Wright Bros., corn millers, acquired these late 18th and 19th century mills. They produced large quantities of flour and 'horse corn' for the Leeds district. In 1991 the buildings were splendidly converted to a high quality hotel.

The business was founded in Keighley in 1828 by the father of John and David Wright, the proprietors of Wright Bros. It was moved to Albion Mills, Garden Street, Leeds, in 1866. The business continued to grow, and was moved to Fletland Mills in 1887. Here the frontage on to the River Aire permitted boats to be discharged and loaded directly, saving the labour of transferring by horse drawn carts to and from the mill and the docks.

There is a long history of milling in Leeds. Domesday Book mentions a mill belonging to the manor of Leeds. In these early times corn milling was a valuable monopoly and a major source of manorial income. When the tenant had gathered in his corn, threshed it and stored it, he was not free to grind it into flour or bake it into bread on his own premises. He was bound to use the lord's corn mill, and the manorial oven. These monopolies, which also extended to the fulling mills, were justified to some extent by the high cost of building and maintaining the mills. The obligation to grind corn at the manorial corn mill in Swinegate (The King's Mills) continued well into the nineteenth century.

In 1815 the *Leeds Intelligencer* carried a notice warning that:

'Whereas divers resiants and inhabitants of the Town of Leeds within the SOKE OF LEEDS OLD MILLS have from time to time neglected to bring their Wheat, Oats, Barley, Peas, Beans, Malt, Pulse etc. to the said Mills to

be ground ... and also have used flour, oatmeal, malt etc. not ground at the said mills. Notice is hereby given that (anyone) found evading the soke ... will have Actions commenced against them. N.B. Any persons using hand mills or querns for the grinding of Corn, crushing of Oats, splitting of beans, peas etc. will be proceeded against.'

This feudal obligation was abolished by Act of Parliament in 1839.

As a result of the huge increase in its population in the nineteenth century, the demand for flour and grains of all types in Leeds was enormous. There were also thousands of horses and farm livestock in Leeds and its vicinity to be fed. Leeds' position on the River Aire and the Leeds & Liverpool Canal made it an ideal location for the wholesaling and processing of grain for distribution to the whole of the West Riding. The grain which came up the waterways was bought and sold in the town's large Corn Exchange and processed at important establishments of which Fletland Mills was a notable example.

The Fletland Mills Plaque was sponsored by Leeds Development Corporation and Mr. Jonathan Wix, the owner of 42 The Calls, and was unveiled by Mr. Keith Roberts, Secretary of the Bransby Agricultural Trading Association, who was then still regularly attending the Corn Exchange, on 25th May 1994. It is at 42, The Calls, Leeds 2.

Joshua Tetley

In 1822 Joshua Tetley bought William Sykes' brewery business which had stood here since 1792. Joshua's enterprise and fine quality ales created a reputation which for over 150 years has made the name 'Tetleys' synonymous with the City of Leeds.

Joshua Tetley was 44 years of age, a married man with seven children, when he took the bold step of purchasing William Sykes' brewery business. He was a member of a sound family business of maltsters in Armley and brandy merchants in the centre of Leeds, and he lived in the high-class residential estate of Park Square. During his first year of owning the business he incurred substantial losses, and moved to a more modest house in the less pleasant district of Salem Place, adjoining the brewery. These and other economies, and sticking to his announced intentions of brewing high quality beer, established the flourishing company.

The first known records of the Tetley family are in the parish register of St. Peter's, Leeds Parish Church, which is a few hundred yards from the famous Tetley brewery. The register records the marriage of George Tetley of Birstal with Easter Dixon of Market Place on 12th April 1681. George and Easter Tetley farmed and owned land at Birkenshaw. They established a family which included a number of maltsters, starting when two of their sons, William and John, started business in Armley.

When Joshua Tetley bought the brewery from their family friend William Sykes, only about 12 per cent of beer sold in Leeds was brewed by common brewers, the rest was brewed by the individual innkeepers. The Beer House Act of 1830 - aimed at discouraging people from drinking gin - allowed anyone paying the two guinea fee to sell beer from their own dwelling. This provided an opportunity to expand brewery sales. The new beer houses had neither the experience nor the equipment to brew beer. The proportion of beer supplied by common breweries almost doubled in ten years, and Joshua Tetley captured a large part of this increased market.

By 1839 the business was solidly established and the family were able to move from the house near the brewery to one of the best residential areas, Belmont, Little Woodhouse. On 1st October 1839 he created Joshua Tetley & Son by taking his son Francis William in to partnership.

The Joshua Tetley Plaque was sponsored by Joshua Tetley and Sons Ltd and unveiled by Mr. Charles Tetley, Great Great Grandson of the brewery founder, Joshua Tetley, on 29th January 1992. It is at The Brewery Gates, Hunslet Road, Leeds 10.

Kirkstall Brewery

Though established in 1833 these magnificent brewery buildings date from the 1860s and 70s. In the late Victorian era the Kirkstall Beer Company exported large quantities of beer to Australia by barge and its own steamships.

Kirkstall Brewery has a somewhat circuitous early history. In 1793 Sir James Graham leased neighbouring plots of land by the Leeds & Liverpool Canal to Henry Cooper and Joseph Musgrave for 300 years. Both men built large maltings on their plots. Joseph Musgrave's maltings were operated by Ephraim Elsworth from 1814 to 1832, after which they passed to Joseph's eldest son, Simeon. In 1833 Thomas Walker of Hunslet purchased these maltings and turned them in to a very well equipped brewery. Walker died bankrupt, and in 1844 the brewery reverted to Simeon Musgrave, who sold it to Benjamin Dawson & Co. Dawson & Co. expanded both the trade and the buildings between 1847 and 1869 in part by buying Henry Cooper's maltings next door and erecting on their site the huge four-storey block familiar to us today.

Benjamin Dawson died in 1869, and the brewery was sold in 1872 to Kirkstall Brewery Company. About this time the brewery was producing 26,000 barrels of beer each year. By 1898 a high tower brewery and new equipment had raised production to 72,000 barrels. These barrels of India Pale Ales, strong ale, mild ale, light bitter, Imperial stout, double stout and porter were not only sold in Leeds and Yorkshire, but also exported. The hogsheads of beer were run out of the arches at water level on to Aire and Calder Navigation Company boats which carried them downstream to Goole, where they were transhipped onto the brewery's own steamships, the 953 ton SS Charante and the 1,831 ton SS Kirkstall of 1895. From Goole these ships commenced the longest beer run in the world, delivering their cargoes to Australia and New Zealand.

In 1936 the brewery was taken over by Dutton's of Blackburn, and in 1954 by Whitbread's of London. They completely re-equipped the plant, and were producing 62,000 barrels of Mackeson stout each year by 1957. Further additions brought the production of bitter and best mild up to 250,000 barrels. Changing tastes and economic circumstances brought a reduction in demand, with the result that the brewery closed in 1983, ending the 150 year tradition of brewing fine beers and stout in Kirkstall valley. In the mid 1990s the buildings were saved for posterity by their imaginative conversion to flats for students of Leeds Metropolitan University.

The Kirkstall Brewery Plaque was sponsored by Leeds Metropolitan University. It is at Broad Road, Leeds 5.

Meanwood Tannery

The monks of Kirkstall Abbey had a water corn mill here in 1230. Milling continued until 1785 when Thomas Martin used the mill for paper-making. In 1857 Samuel Smith built this fine tannery. From 1911 to 1994 it was used as a fellmongery.

A remarkable feature of Victorian Leeds was the rapid growth of the local leather industry. As the late-Georgian population had mushroomed, the demand for footwear had risen. Skins and hides had been eagerly purchased from the town's butchers, but soon supplies had to be supplemented from India. The Leeds leather industry grew rapidly between 1850 and 1880 with large tanneries being built in particular in the Buslingthorpe, Meanwood and Kirkstall districts. Meanwood Tannery had a long and fascinating history.

A Kirkstall Abbey charter of 1230 refers to a pond and mill at LeMenewde, and the water mill is referred to in later records. Ralph Thoresby's *Ducatus Leodiensis* (1715) refers to Mr. Walker's corn mill at Headingley Moor, and a 1766 deed refers to all those two water corn mills commonly called Wood Mills consisting of two water wheels, two pairs of grey stones and one pair of blue stones and other equipment and 20 acres all in Chapel Allerton. In 1785 Peter Garforth, executor of Thomas Garforth, leased the mills to Thomas Martin, paper maker. (Thomas Martin was the great great grandfather of the late Sir George Martin of Adel and Leeds, who was one of the founder members of Leeds Civic Trust.)

In 1856 the mills and land were purchased by Samuel Smith, and converted into a large tannery. Samuel was a member of the family of Leeds butchers who had slaughter houses off Briggate on the site of the County Arcade. The tannery was the chief support of the inhabitants of the village of Meanwood, where the firm were the main landowners. It was one of the largest in the kingdom. Most of the five acre site was covered with large buildings, including 300 pits capable of holding several hundred thousand gallons of tanning liquid and about 70,000 hides.

Samuel Smith senior was the brother of John Smith who set up the brewery in Tadcaster in 1847. When Samuel died in 1880 his son Samuel was 18 years old; three years later he became the proprietor. In 1889, when Samuel's younger brother William became 21, he joined with Samuel and the firm became known as Messrs. S. & W. Smith.

The business continued until 1891 when Harold Nichols leased the tannery. Tanning ceased on the site in 1904. From 1911 to 1994 the premises were used as a fellmongery, first by Meanwood Fellmongers, later by Jowitt & Son, Fellmongers, Robert Barker & Son Ltd, and then FMC Products Ltd. In 1998 the tannery was saved from demolition by conversion to flats.

The Meanwood Tannery Plaque was sponsored by Country & Metropolitan Homes Northern Ltd and was unveiled by Mr. Fred Casperson and Mr. Arthur Hopwood, distinguished local historians, on 17th July 1999. It is at Millpond Road, off Monksbridge Road, Meanwood, Leeds 6.

Cliff Tannery

These magnificently renovated buildings, now known as Sugarwell Court, were built by Edward Kitchen, in 1866, as the Cliff Tannery and Leather Works. As a premier member of the large Victorian Leeds leather industry, it specialised in East India Kips and Cape and Sydney butts.

Edward Kitchin & Sons, Tanners, Curriers and Leather Factors was founded by Mr. Edward Kitchin in 1840. He had a tanner's and currier's premises in Harper Street, Leeds, and commenced the tanning department at Meanwood in the mid 1850s. Kitchin acquired ten acres of land in Meanwood Road in 1862, and in 1866 Cliff Tannery and Leather Works was built. Sixty-three cottages were erected on the site for the benefit of their workpeople, and the partnership also owned a substantial warehouse in Basinghall Street, Leeds.

Edward's son, Frederick Conyers Kitchin was taken in to partnership in 1867 and was responsible for developing the successful factoring side of the business. Matthew Kitchin joined his father and brother as a partner in 1873, and became responsible for the tannery in Meanwood Road.

In 1894 shortly after Edward's death, the partnership was dissolved. Frederick Conyers Kitchin continued the business of Edward Kitchin & Sons as leather factors, and Matthew Kitchin took over the tannery in Meanwood Road.

Although eventually much of the leather industry in Leeds was based on imported hides - Kitchin's specialities were East India Kips and Cape and Sydney butts - the leather industry in Leeds serves as a good example of how strong inter-relationships between local industries promoted their growth. The principal raw materials were cattle and horsehides, calfskins and sheepskins, initially obtained in large measure from the town's slaughterhouses. The local chemical industry was stimulated because, besides gambier and shumac and other tanning agents, cod oil, acid, lime and various dyewares, were also required. By-products of the trade included refuse hair, used in the manufacture of cheap carpets and blankets, and scrapings for the glue industry, whilst spent lime and solids from the tanpits were sold to local farmers for manure. In all some 20,000 people were said to depend directly or indirectly upon the leather trade by the 1860s.

The Cliff Tannery Plaque was sponsored by Leeds Metropolitan University. It is near the entrance to Sugarwell Court, Meanwood Road, Leeds 7.

THE BUILDING IS NOW IN USE AS A STUDENT RESIDENCE

Burmantofts Pottery

1842 - 1957

Coal mining and brick making began here in 1842. From 1880, using the site's fireclay, Wilcock & Co made terracotta and glazed coloured Burmantofts Faience for flower pot stands, ornaments and decorative bricks and tiles used in buildings all over the world.

Burmantofts (burgage-men's tofts) is so named because it was here that the tenants of the 60 or more burgage plots created on either side of Briggate in 1207 had their allotments - or tofts. These allotments, where they could grow food, were a privilege granted to them by the Lord of the Manor of Leeds. In the seventeenth century it was a very desirable suburban area. Burmantofts Hall was built at the end of the seventeenth century for Sir William Neville, High Sheriff of Yorkshire. It was situated near Burmantofts Street and St. Mary's Lane, and was described as standing in the forest and meadows surrounded by gardens and orchards.

From 1842 the coal deposits found 30 feet below the surface of the ground at Burmantofts were mined by Wilcock and Co who supplied domestic coal. The large beds of good quality fire clay also found here enabled the firm to expand into the manufacture of bricks, sanitary pipes, chimney pots, fire-backs and other clay products. By the 1870s the work occupied about 4 acres, and had an output of 90,000 bricks per week. From the 1880s the firm found fame with the production of glazed coloured tiles and shaped bricks, the renowned 'Burmantofts Faience' ideal for smoky

Victorian cities, as well as a wide range of plain and terracotta tiles and bricks. To these was added an extensive range of beautifully coloured faience vases, flower pot stands, plaques and ornaments of all sorts.

At its height the company employed 700 people and the works covered 16 acres. The works closed in 1957, and the land became used for a Council housing estate.

There are many notable buildings in Leeds where Burmantofts faience and terracotta were used, including County Arcade, Briggate (interior and exterior); Leeds University Great Hall; Scottish Union Offices, Park Row; Thornton & Co Premises, Briggate; and the School of Medicine, Thoresby Place. Burmantofts products were used in virtually all the important towns in the United Kingdom, and were also exported for use overseas, including buildings in Paris, Montreal, Shanghai, St. Petersburg, Australia, America, Greece and India.

The Burmantofts Pottery Plaque was sponsored by Bramall Construction and unveiled by George Mudie M.P. on 10th December 1999. It is at Gargrave Court, off Gargrave Approach, Leeds 9.

Louis Le Prince

Louis Aime Augustin Le Prince came to Leeds in 1866 where he experimented in cinematography. In 1888 he patented a one-lens camera with which he filmed Leeds Bridge from this British Waterways building. These were probably the world's first successful moving pictures.

SIR RICHARD ATTENBOROUGH AT THE UNVEILING

The unveiling of this plaque on the 13th October 1988 by Mr. William Le Prince Huettle of Memphis, Tennessee, a great grandson of Louis Le Prince marked the 100th anniversary of the world's first moving pictures being filmed.

The short clip of film taken in October 1888 was shown at the Le Prince International Film Festival in Leeds held in October 1988. It shows horse drawn wagons and pedestrians crossing the bridge in the autumn sunshine. Le Prince's colleague James Longley wrote 'It was as if you were on the bridge yourself. I could even see the smoke coming out of a man's pipe, who was lounging on the bridge.'

Louis Le Prince was born in Metz, France in 1842. His father was a Major in the French Army, and was a close friend of Daguerre, a pioneer of photography. Louis Le Prince was the subject of a Daguerrotype, and also had lessons from Daguerre. His education included the study of painting in Paris and postgraduate chemistry at Leipzig University provided him with the academic knowledge to persue his consuming ambition of achieving the production of moving pictures. He moved to Leeds in 1866 to join his college friend John Whitley in Whitley Partners of Hunslet, a firm of brass founders making valves and components. In 1869 he married

Elizabeth Whitley, John's sister, who was a talented artist. They started a school of applied art in Park Street, Leeds. The Le Princes became famous for their work in fixing colour photography on to metal and pottery, and gained a commission for portraits of Queen Victoria and Gladstone produced in this way to be placed with other mementos of the time in a time capsule

LOUIS LE PRINCE

The Pioneer of cinematography had a workshop on this site where he invented a one-lens camera and a projecting machine. Le Prince produced what are believed to be the world's first moving pictures taken on Leeds Bridge in 1888.

Camera was described in the British Patent of 10th October 1888 in the section that read 'When the receiver is provided with only one lens as it sometimes might be, it is so constructed that the sensitive film is intermittently operated at the rear of the said lens which is provided with a properly timed intermittent shutter; and correspondingly in the deliverer (projector) when only one lens is provided the band of ribbon or transparencies is automatically so operated as to bring the pictures intermittently and in the proper order of succession opposite the said lens.' At this point Le Prince had achieved all the necessary factors for the taking and projection of moving pictures. He was the first to make a successful camera to take pictures at over 16 frames per second; the first exhibitor of moving pictures - on a screen in Leeds in 1888 - and he was the first to use the method of registering the moving of the pictures by perforations and sprocket wheels.

In September 1890 Le Prince went to France with Mr. and Mrs Richard Wilson of Leeds. He left them on a Friday with the promise that he would rejoin them in Paris on the following Monday for the return journey to England, before he set off for America with his invention. Le Prince did not arrive at the appointed time, nor was he ever seen again by his family and friends. All that could be established was that he was seen boarding a train at Dijon for his return to Paris on September 16th 1890.

Thomas Alva Edison invented the phonograph in 1877, and commissioned Dickson, a young laboratory assistant, to invent a motion picture camera as a visual accompaniment for it. This was patented in 1893. Equally, it was some five years after the presumed death of Le Prince that the Cinematograph of the Lumiere Brothers appeared as the first viable machine for taking and projecting motion pictures. Louis Le Prince therefore may justly be called the true pioneer of cinematography.

(manufactured by Whitley Partners of Hunslet) which was placed in the foundations of Cleopatra's Needle on the Thames Embankment.

In 1881 Louis Le Prince went to America as an agent for Whitley's , and at the end of his contract he and his family stayed in that country. Louis became manager of a group of French Artists who produced large panoramas, (usually of famous battles), for exhibition in New York, Washington and Chicago. During this time he continued his experiments for a means of producing moving photographs and to find the best material for films.

Whilst Louis Le Prince was in America he built a camera with sixteen lenses, which was the subject of his first patent. Although this camera was capable of photographing motion it did not achieve perfect success because each lens photographed the image from a slightly different viewpoint, and the projected image jumped about. Le Prince returned to Leeds in 1886 where he built and patented his successful one-lens camera. In Leeds he was supported by his father-in-law Joseph Whitley, James Wm. Longley, Frederick Mason and his son Adolphe. The Le Prince Single Lens

The first Louis Le Prince plaque was sponsored by British Waterways Board and was unveiled by William Le Prince Huettle, great grandson of Louis Le Prince on 13th October 1988. It is at British Waterways, Leeds Bridge, Lower Briggate, Leeds LS1.

The second Louis Le Prince Plaque was sponsored by British Broadcasting Corporation and unveiled by Sir Richard Attenborough, actor, broadcaster and film director, Patron, Leeds Film Festival, on 14th October 1988. It is on the BBC Studios, Woodhouse Lane, Leeds 2.

Joseph Aspdin

1778 - 1855

Portland Cement, one of mankind's most important manufactured materials, was patented by Joseph Aspdin, a Leeds bricklayer, on 21 October 1824. Aspdin lived in this yard (then called Slip Inn Yard) and first sold his cement in Angel Inn Yard.

LECTURE THEATRE BLOCK, CHANCELLOR'S COURT, LEEDS UNIVERSITY (1960s). CONSTRUCTED IN CONCRETE OF WHICH PORTLAND CEMENT IS AN ESSENTIAL PART.

The firm suffered a setback in the late 1840s when the Wakefield factory was demolished because it was in the path of a new railway line, and a new factory was built at Ings Road, Wakefield.

Joseph Aspdin married Mary Fotherby in 1811 and they had two sons, William, born in 1813 and James, born in 1814, and four daughters, Caroline, Mary, Charlotte and Louisa. The family lived at 3, Princess Street, New Road, Leeds, and later moved to Wakefield. His grave is in St. John's churchyard, Wakefield.

When Joseph Aspdin's father, Thomas Aspdin, died in 1800 Joseph became largely responsible for bringing up his two brothers and sister. His father had been a bricklayer, and Joseph followed on in that trade.

In his search and experiments for an improved cement Aspdin may have been influenced by John Smeaton the famous Leeds Civil Engineer who did a great deal of research into materials that would harden under water before building the Eddystone Lighthouse. It is reported that Aspdin was fined for taking limestone off the roads, which he found useful because it was ground to so fine a powder by the traffic. When Aspdin achieved success he named the material Portland Cement because of its resemblance, when set, to a limestone from the Isle of Portland. It was manufactured by burning and finely grinding a mixture of limestone and clay, or limestone and shale.

After patenting the results of all his experiments in 1824, Aspdin took a partner, and in 1828 Aspdin and Beverley, makers of Portland Cement had premises at 68 Briggate Leeds and at Kirkgate, Wakefield. The high quality of Portland Cement became recognised, and it was used by Sir Mark Isambard Brunel in the building of the Thames Tunnel between Rotherhithe and Wapping, which was completed in 1841.

The Joseph Aspdin Plaque was sponsored by the British Cement Association and unveiled by Sir George Moseley, Chairman of the British Cement Association and Chairman of the National Civic Trust, on 21st October 1994. It is at Packhorse Yard, between Lands Lane and Briggate, Leeds 1.

JOSEPH ASPDIN
(1778 ~ 1855)

Portland Cement, one of mankind's most important manufactured materials, was patented by Joseph Aspdin, a Leeds Bricklayer, on 21 October 1824. Aspdin lived in this yard (then called Slip Inn Yard) and first sold his cement in Angel Inn Yard.

Oakwood Clock

The Oakwood Clock was made in 1904 by Potts and Sons, to the design of Leeming and Leeming as the centrepiece of the new Leeds Market Hall. Alterations to the Market led to the inspired decision to erect the clock at Oakwood in 1912.

*T*he Century's Progress: Yorkshire Industry and Commerce, 1893 noted 'William Potts & Sons, Clock Manufacturers to H.M. Home and Colonial Governments and the Principal Railway Companies, 12 and 13, Guildford Street Leeds. Rarely is it given to one individual firm to attain such wide repute and identity with a single branch of industry as that which has been acquired by the famous Leeds firm whose operations have placed them at the head of the English clockmaking industry and trade.'

William Potts was born in Darlington in 1809, the son of Robert Potts, an established clockmaker. William was apprenticed to Samuel Thompson, who, like his father was a well-known Darlington clockmaker. In 1832 he moved to Pudsey and founded his own business as a domestic clockmaker and repairer of clocks and watches. He soon became interested in the growing demand for the maintenance and supply of public clocks and gained many commissions.

The list of clocks made by Potts for prestige buildings is most impressive - cathedrals, town halls, churches, universities, banks, commercial and industrial premises, and numerous railway stations and railway buildings in the north of England. The firm must have made hundreds of wall clocks. Before 1930 all Leeds schools had them, as did public buildings and hospitals where reliability and accuracy in time-keeping was important.

More than a hundred public clocks of the tower clock type were installed in Leeds buildings between 1862 and 1933.

Perhaps the best known Potts clocks in Leeds now are those in Thornton's Arcade and the Grand Arcade. The Thornton's Arcade clock made in 1877 has Cambridge quarter chimes, a cast iron dial and five bells. The hammers are concealed at the back of the bells which appear to be struck by the J. W. Appleyard figures representing Friar Tuck, Richard Coeur de Lyon, Robin Hood and Garth the swine herd. The scene is from Sir Walter Scott's Ivanhoe.

In the days before wrist watches became common public clocks played a very important part in daily life. Oakwood Clock has been a famous Leeds landmark and a meeting place for generations of Leeds people.

The Oakwood Clock Plaque was sponsored by William H Brown, estate agents and unveiled by Sir James Savile, TV celebrity and local resident, on 7th April 1998. It is at 498 Roundhay Road, Leeds 8.

Samuel Smiles

1812 - 1905

The great propagandist of Victorian values through his books 'Self-Help', 'Character', 'Thrift' and 'Duty' inspired by his lectures to Leeds working men in 1845. He lived in Leeds 1838-58 as a newspaper editor, doctor and then railway secretary.

FORMER TEMPERANCE HALL AND MECHANICS INSTITUTE, HOLBORN APPROACH, LEEDS 6.

Samuel Smiles was born in Haddington, Berwickshire, on 23rd December 1812, one of eleven children. His father died in 1832, the same year that Smiles qualified in medicine in Edinburgh. He soon abandoned medical practice for journalism, and moved to Leeds where he edited the progressive and reformist *Leeds Times* from 1838 to 1842. From 1845 to 1866 he was employed in railway administration, first as secretary of the Leeds and Thirsk Railway.

As an ardent social and political reformer, Smiles was keen to advance the condition of the working classes. He sought to do this in particular by improving their education and encouraging them through his books. To this end he was the founder of the Temperance Hall and Mechanics Institute in Woodhouse built in 1850 on what is now known as Holborn Approach. Dr. Smiles and his friends gave free lessons in reading and writing to adults, and they provided a library.

In 1857 he published a life of the inventor and founder of the railways, George Stephenson. He followed this with the best selling book *Self-Help: with Illustrations of*

Character and Conduct, the outcome of a series of lectures on self-improvement given to young men in Leeds. This was a huge success, selling over 250,000 copies by 1900. It was translated into many foreign languages and even provided mottoes for the Khedive's palace in Egypt. In this he wrote 'A penny is a very small matter, yet the comfort of thousands of families depends upon the proper spending and saving of pennies. If a man allows the little pennies, the results of his hard work, to slip out of his fingers - some to the beer shop, some this way and some that - he will find that his life is little raised above one of mere animal drudgery. On the other hand, if he takes care of the pennies - putting some weekly into a benefit society - this money will represent many things of great value; not only food, clothing, and household satisfaction, but personal self-respect and independence.'

In recognition of Smiles' support for working men's education our plaque is placed on the Leeds Mechanics' Institute, where he lectured in later life. The Institute was founded in 1825, and in 1842 the Leeds Literary Society joined with it to become the Leeds Mechanics Institution and Literary Society. In 1897 the title was changed to The Leeds Institute of Science Art and Literature. Today's Mechanics Institute building on Cookridge Street was designed by Cuthbert Brodrick, and opened in 1868 It became the Civic Theatre on Friday 7th October 1949.

The Samuel Smiles Plaque was sponsored by The Leeds & Holbeck Building Society and unveiled by Mr. J. Olav Arnold, President of Leeds Civic Trust, on 29th March 1994. It is at The Leeds Institute, and Civic Theatre, Cookridge Street, Leeds 2.

TRANSPORT

Excellent transport facilities have been of critical importance to the growth and success of Leeds industry and commerce. In the seventeenth and eighteenth centuries when road communications were very poor, the Leeds merchant community was desperately keen to turn Leeds into an inland port by making the River Aire navigable to Hull. This was achieved in 1700 and the trade of the town flourished. In the 1770s Leeds businessmen had both the audacity and the vision to back the concept of a canal stretching all the way across the Pennines from Leeds to Liverpool. When this was completed in 1816, combined with the Aire and Calder Navigation, Leeds was at the hub of a waterway network reaching right across the country—the M62 motorway of its day. The commercial advantages were enormous. The barges of the river and canal brought in large quantities of stone, coal, timber, grain and the many necessities of life vital to Leeds and its hinterland, and took away many of the products it produced and sold to the United Kingdom and the wider world.

In 1834 the opening of the Leeds to Selby line brought the Railway Age to Leeds. While the waterways continued to prosper, Leeds soon became a major railway centre. The separate efforts of a number of important railway companies created the inconvenience of competing town-centre railway stations and the lack of direct links between track serving important destinations. At the price of an enormous visual impact on the town centre, the most major anomaly was remedied in 1869 when the North-Eastern Railway Viaduct was opened linking Marsh Lane Station and the 'New Station' next to Wellington Station (where City Station now stands).

Both the waterways and particularly the railways provided a great deal of employment in Leeds. In the later years when many trade unions were being formed, the importance of Leeds as a railway centre was recognised when in 1881 Holbeck was chosen as the place for the first registered office of the Associated Society of Locomotive Engineers and Firemen (A.S.L.E.& F.).

Aire and Calder Navigation

Before the railway age, the making navigable of the River Aire importantly made Leeds an inland port connected directly to Hull. Cheap water carriage was vital for the successful export of the cloth marketed and finished in the town. The Aire and Calder was opened in 1700.

The merchants of Leeds finally overcame centuries of opposition from York when, with the help of Wakefield merchants, they obtained Parliament's consent in 1699 to construct the Aire and Calder Navigation. This established Leeds as a major inland port, with direct links to London, the Netherlands and the Baltic trade through the Humber and the port of Hull. Up to this time Leeds merchants had to send their cloth by road 'having no conveniency of water carriage within sixteen miles of them, which not only occasions great expence, but many times great damage to their goods, and sometimes the roads are impassable.' The nearest wharves were at Rawcliffe, where the river Don joins the Aire, at Selby, a few miles south of the junction of the river Wharfe with the river Ouse, and at Goole, further down the Ouse.

after heavy rain. In August 1767 the river level rose six feet in a single hour. A thirty-six hour deluge in October 1775 left the whole riverside under water: 'large quantities of grain deposited in Warehouses were washed away, cloth in some places torn from the tenters, in others the cloth and tenters were carried away together; several dwelling houses and dye-houses suffered greatly, dyeing vats being torn out of their places; the pavement in the streets broken up; walls thrown down; cows, horses and sheep forced into the water and drowned.' By a further Act of 1774, new navigable channels were cut alongside the river at Knostrop and Thwaite, about a mile downstream, improving the passage of vessels up and down the Navigation. In 1778 a canal was opened from Haddlesey to Selby, linking the Aire and Calder

LEEDS WATERFRONT IN 1827. THE NAVIGATION WAREHOUSE WAS DESTROYED BY FIRE AND DEMOLISHED. ONLY THE ORIGINAL BASE COURSE ARCHES REMAIN BELOW TODAY'S RESIDENTIAL DEVELOPMENT.

By clearing a number of obstacles, and building a series of weirs and locks to deepen the water at various points, the Aire was made navigable. Similarly the Calder was made navigable from Wakefield to where it flowed into the Aire at Castleford. From November 1700 boats could sail from the Humber to Leeds Bridge, where a new Town's Warehouse had been erected on the northern bank.

One of the main problems of using the natural course of the river for navigation was the liability of flooding

Navigation with the Ouse. This was followed by five new cuts eliminating difficult stretches of the river. The result of these works was that Selby became the principal eastern terminus of the Navigation.

The Aire and Calder Navigation Plaque was sponsored by Tay Homes and British Waterways and unveiled by Mr. Norman Stubbs Chief Executive, Tay Homes, on 20th April 1993. It is at Riverside Court, Call Lane, Leeds 1.

Leeds and Liverpool Canal Warehouse

In 1777 this robust stone building was constructed as a terminal warehouse for the Leeds and Liverpool Canal. Started in 1770, the canal was finally completed in 1816 at a cost of £1,200,000 - nearly five times the original estimate.

The success of the Duke of Bridgewater's canal from Worsley Mill to Manchester prompted a Halifax man, Mr. John Longbotham, to propose a scheme for a canal to link Leeds and Liverpool. A meeting of interested merchants and landowners called in James Brindley to survey the proposed line. In December 1768 Brindley reported that the scheme was practicable.

It was an extraordinary venture: Joseph Priestley, the chief clerk and land agent of the Aire and Calder Navigation, writing half a century later noted that 'At that era of canal navigation, when first commenced, it was one of the boldest and most magnificent projects hitherto attempted in Great Britain.' Indeed, contemporaries marvelled at the length of the canal but much more awesome was the mountainous landscape which had to be negotiated between the two towns. The difference between the water levels at Leeds Bridge and the canal basin at North Lady's Walk in Liverpool was a mere 21 feet but in its eventual course of 127 miles the canal climbed 411 feet over undulating terrain necessitating 844 feet of lockage, 8 aqueducts, a massive embankment two-thirds of a mile long and over one-and-a-quarter miles of tunnel.

Strictly speaking the canal commenced at Leeds Bridge where the jurisdiction of the Aire and Calder Navigation ended. In practice it began at its first lock to the west of Victoria Bridge, where the canal company's main warehouse and other extensive warehouses, wharves, basins and docks were situated.

In May 1770 an Act of Parliament was obtained by which the 529 subscribers became incorporated as 'The Company of Proprietors of the Canal Navigation from Leeds to Liverpool'. The Company was empowered to raise £260,000 in £100 shares, with the option to raise a further £60,000 later. Construction began at both ends in July 1770, and in 1775 a 28 mile section from Liverpool to Newburgh was opened for trade. On 4th June 1777 a 33 mile section from Leeds to Holmbridge near Gargrave was also opened for trade. Although construction work was then abandoned for 13 years the sections opened were used and provided a much needed link between Leeds and the clothing district to its west.

Further Acts of Parliament were obtained, in 1790 to permit more finance to be raised, and in 1794 to permit modifications to the route. The canal was completed with the opening of the Blackburn to Wigan link in October 1816. It provided great economic benefit to the country through which it passed.

The Leeds and Liverpool Canal Warehouse Plaque was sponsored by Mr. Len Davis of Leeds Canal Basin (Development) Ltd., developer of Granary Wharf, and unveiled by him on 3rd May 1990. It is at the Canal Basin, Water Lane, Leeds 11.

North - Eastern Railway Viaduct

This 1500 yard viaduct, including the New Station (now known as City Station) built over the river and canal, is one of the great feats of Victorian civil engineering. Erected between 1866 and 1869, it linked railway termini on opposite sides of Leeds.

The Leeds newspapers reported that on 1st April 1869 the North-Eastern Railway Company completed an undertaking which would rank amongst the many great engineering feats in the annals of railway enterprise. The benefits to passengers and shareholders of this expensive provision of new terminus accommodation and direct rail links were detailed in lengthy reports. The viaduct linked Marsh Lane Station and the railway lines on the east side of the town to the lines on the west side. It thereby enabled the company to use its own lines to link its extensive

hundreds of houses along the line.'

The line of the viaduct effectively cut Leeds in two, and inhibited the development south of the arches for the next hundred years. Where it cut through the burial ground of St. Peter's, Leeds Parish Church, which had been rebuilt and re-opened in 1838, it was thought more correct to cover the graves with an embankment rather than to excavate them to provide footings for arches. The gravestones are displayed on the side of this short embankment.

rail network through the industrial and commercial areas of northern England to both the eastern and western coastal resorts and ports.

The report noted that in the excavation for the eastern abutment of the bridge between Call Lane and Briggate three of the old bell ironstone pits which the Romans were supposed to have worked were brought to light. Here a man was killed 'That such was the only serious accident may be considered exceedingly fortunate, considering the danger attendant on pulling down

The development of Granary Wharf has provided better access to visit the 'Dark Arches' which are one of the most interesting architectural features of central Leeds.

The North-Eastern Railway Viaduct Plaque was sponsored by Leeds Corporation and British Rail's Community Unit and unveiled by Mr. Gerald Egan, Leeds City Station Manager, on 27th April 1993. It is at the Swinegate end of the Viaduct, Leeds 1.

A.S.L.E. & F.

The Associated Society of Locomotive Engineers and Firemen was founded in 1880. Because of the convenience and importance of Leeds as a railway centre, the Society established its first registered office here at the Commercial Inn, Sweet Street in 1881.

The Associated Society of Locomotive Engineers and Firemen was formed by a small group of members in Sheffield in 1880. A second branch was formed in Leeds, and in 1881 the union held its first Annual Conference at the Commercial Inn on Sweet Street in Holbeck. The union's first national executive and general secretary were elected there and the Commercial became its headquarters. Ten years later the headquarters were moved to 44 Park Square, Leeds, and in 1926 to their present home at 9 Arkwright Road, Hampstead, London.

The first rule book specified that: 'The objects of this Society shall be to form funds, by entrance fees and weekly contributions, for the relief of its members in sickness, incapacitation by old age or accident, from following their profession or calling, by paying a sum of money at death of members or their wives, and for the relief or maintenance of the members when on travel in search of employment, or when in distressed circumstances, and to advance the interests of its members in their various professions and callings by procuring a reduction in the excessive hours of labour, regulating the speed of trains, the adoption of modern improvements for the general safe working over all railways in the United Kingdom, and generally in such other manner and to such extent as the Executive Committee may determine.'

The first railway, as we now understand the term, carrying all traffic by steam traction between cities, with a form of fixed signalling, was the Liverpool and Manchester railway. Built and engined by George Stephenson, it was opened on 15th September 1830. The end of the 1830s saw the first of the great British main lines, linking London with Lancashire, Bristol and Southampton. From 1845/6 dates the great expansion of railways over most of Britain.

When George Stephenson asserted that he could run passenger coaches at 12 to 15 miles an hour he was regarded as an optimist. Speeds rapidly increased, on 11th May 1848 the G.W.R. Bristol express ran from Paddington to Didcot, fifty-three and a half miles, in a running time of 47 minutes from start to stop, an average of 68 miles an hour. On 31st August 1888 the Great North East Coast Express travelled the 400 miles from London to Edinburgh in 7 hours 27 minutes, and speeds of up to 75 m.p.h. were achieved. It is not surprising that the drivers were very concerned about safety!

The A. S. L. E. & F. Plaque was sponsored by A. S. L. E .& F. and unveiled by Mr. Derrick Fullick, General Secretary (of A.S.L.E. & F.) on 17th January 1991. It is at The Commercial Inn, Sweet Street, Leeds 11.

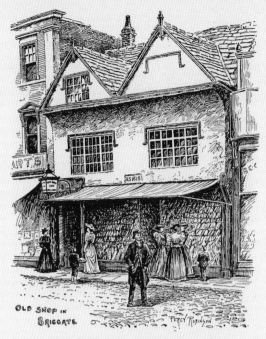

RICHARD SYKES' HOUSE BUILT 1615

HOUSES

Well into the eighteenth century the well-to-do woollen merchant and professional classes and the 'lower orders' were content to live alongside one another in the central streets of Leeds. In the middle of the seventeenth century visitors to Leeds were generally unimpressed by its 'ancient meane and lowe built timber-framed houses' and noted that 'only some fewe of the richer sort of the Inhabitants have theire houses more large and capacious'.

In the late seventeenth and early eighteenth centuries, however, the growing wealth of the woollen merchants enabled them to build fine town houses, of the kind illustrated in the borders of Cossins' Plan of Leeds of 1726, in Briggate, Kirkgate and Boar Lane close to the cloth markets. The population grew to around 6,000 by 1700 and 16,000 by the 1770s. Since no new streets were built, the burgeoning ranks of the lower orders were accommodated by building cottages in the yards and orchards behind the principal street frontages.

The significant move to the residential segregation of the different classes began in the late 1760s when the development of the exclusively middle-class Park Estate on the western edge of the town centre began. At the same time genteel villas started to be built in numbers on the pleasant northern slope of Little Woodhouse close to the town. The very rich built mansion houses in sizable estates, Benjamin Gott at Armley, John Marshall at the New Grange (now Beckett's Park) and the Brown's, the woollen merchants, out at what later became known as Potternewton.

The onset of the Industrial Revolution, with the dramatic rise in the town's population to almost 90,000 by 1840, brought the further cramming of the working classes into the town centre yards. Added to this was the building of thousands of back-to-back houses to the east of Briggate and, by the early decades of the nineteenth century, at Quarry Hill, the Bank, Holbeck and Hunslet and in the roadside fields to the north of the town centre.

As the factory smoke blew from the west, and environmental conditions deteriorated in the overcrowded and insanitary town centre, the wealthier middle classes began to abandon the Park Estate and head for villas in the 'New Leeds', today referred to as Chapeltown and Harehills, and in Headingley. But not everyone wanted a large villa so far from town. Clarendon Road gained many fine houses in the Victorian period, Fairbairn House being perhaps the grandest of them all.

Queens Court

This historic courtyard occupies one of the 60 burgage plots which abutted Briggate in the Middle Ages. It is fronted by an eight-bayed woollen cloth merchant's house (built c.1714) and contains the merchant's cloth finishing shops and warehouses.

Queens Court is a marvellous example of how one of the historic Briggate yards has been refurbished and brought back into use. The woollen cloth merchant's house, which marks its frontage, is a rare surviving example of the large houses which were built on Briggate in the early eighteenth century when the cloth market was in its heyday. It was almost certainly the home of the Oates, one of the great eighteenth century merchant families. The court itself contains original eighteenth and nineteenth century cloth merchants' finishing shops and warehouses.

In 1853 the main frontage of Queens Court appears to have been in two occupations; number 167 was occupied by Sidney and Stables, Tea Dealers, and number 168 by Sarah Johnson, Linen and Woollen Draper. The yard itself was occupied by no less than seven different traders. *White's 1853 Leeds Directory* lists them as: John Naylor & Co., Woollen Cloth Merchant also of Westgate Common, Wakefield; Samuel Smith of Meanwood, Tanner and Leather Dealer; Thomas Royston, Flock Dealer of 7, Queen's Court; Berendt and Levy, Woolstaplers and Merchants, wool, hair and shoddy importers, of 8, Queen's Court and Hamburgh;

Thomas Richardson, Drysalter and Manufacturing Chemist of 10, Queen's Court; Thomas Etches, Soap and Oil Merchant of 11, Queen's Court; Moxon & Walker, Printers and Stationers of 18, Queen's Court.

Samuel Smith of Meanwood (see page 23) was one of the major firms involved in the important leather industry in Leeds. They attended the leather fairs held at Leeds South Market which was built in 1823 -1826, the first quarterly leather fair being held there on 17th October 1827. The South Market, between Hunslet Lane and Meadow Lane was essentially a market place with extensive covered facilities. The whole area included 23 butchers' shops and stalls, 26 miscellaneous shops, 88 stalls, 9 slaughterhouses and 18 dwellings. By 1868 the South Market Leather Fair had become the largest leather market outside London, illustrating the rapid growth of the leather industry in Leeds. In 1871, 23 tanneries and 60 curriers employed about 2000 people. Samuel Smith would find Queen's Court a convenient place to store hides and leather products before and after the leather sales, and for easy despatch on the river.

The area appears to have been a centre for leather traders, as immediately south of Queen's Court is Saddle Yard where William Law, Leather Factor, traded. Law also traded at 172 Briggate, next door to the Saddle Hotel, and Charles Watson & Son, Currier and Leather Cutters were at 47 Call Lane.

The Queens Court Plaque was sponsored by Mr. Brian Prideaux, property developer, who was responsible for the restoration of Queens Court, and unveiled by him on 2nd May 1990.It is at Queens Court, Lower Briggate, Leeds 1.

18 Park Place

This house, restored to its former grandeur by M E P C plc in 1988, is situated in one of the most elegant streets of Georgian Leeds. Merchants and gentlemen were attracted here by the then beautiful view of the river and neighbouring hills. Erected 1788.

During the mid eighteenth century the Wilson family in Leeds inherited from the Sykes family a large area of park land running from the old Leeds turnpike to the River Aire, covering an area which is today the legal and financial area of Leeds city centre. The family decided to develop the land as a high-class residential area on the lines of Bath or Bloomsbury. The first thoroughfare to be developed was Park Row in 1767-76 and this was followed by East Parade, and South Parade, and then Park Place and Park Square.

When 18 Park Place, called Park House, was built in 1788 it was part of a terrace, and the most striking architecturally with its grand pediment and six large pilasters with classical capitals. It was like the building at the Adelphi, London, designed by the Adams brothers. It was a very desirable residence in what was then a new and exclusive part of Leeds. To the rear of the building was a graceful Georgian square and, from the front windows, could be seen the River Aire graced by farms and woodland on both banks. *The Leeds Guide* of 1806 said of Park Place: 'all the houses are built in a very superior style, and are principally inhabited by affluent merchants or gentlemen who have retired from business. The promenade in Park Place is without exception one of the most pleasing in the town'. Following the sale of the Kirkgate Vicarage and croft in the 1820s, the Vicarage of Leeds was in Park Place, and amongst others who lived there were Dr. Walter Hook and Canon Woodford.

After Richard Wilson died in 1794, leaving the estate to his brothers Thomas and Christopher, a plot of land on the west side was sold for the building of a large factory, from which the prevailing wind blew smoke and other noxious fumes across the elegant terraces.

John Atkinson of Little Woodhouse, giving evidence to the Select Committee on Smoke Prevention in 1845 stated: 'Park Place and Park Square, which used to be the residences of the best families in Leeds, have been gradually desecrated for several years past in consequence of the increased smoke.....The houses there are too large for persons of moderate means, and are too smoky for those who could live in them. They are in the best part of Leeds but the parties are driven out of town; they live a mile or two out of town now; and as they have means of omnibuses they can do it. They used to live near their businesses.'

After being owned by five families 18 Park Place was sold for commercial development in 1865, and since that date until the property company MEPC's purchase of the building in 1973, the property was used mainly in connection with the clothing trade.

The 18 Park Place Plaque was sponsored by MEPC plc and unveiled by Sir Christopher Benson, Chairman of MEPC on 24th February 1989. It is at 18, Park Place, Leeds 1.

Park Square

This elegant square formed part of the Wilson family's plan to create a high-class residential estate on the site of the medieval park of the Manor of Leeds. Its residents were merchants, clergy, lawyers and surgeons. Built 1788 - 1810

Leeds was a dynamic town in the period that the Park Estate was being developed. The population doubled between 1775 and 1811, and had doubled again by 1831, increasing from 30,609 to 123,548 in 56 years. During this period the town's economy was broadening from being based on the merchanting and distribution of woollen textiles from small manufacturing units, to one which included big textile mills producing woollens, linens, worsteds, and cottons, and the engineering and leather industries.

The faltering nature of the Wilson's ambitions to develop the Park Estate is well demonstrated by the spasmodic development of Park Square. Though begun in 1788 it was twenty-two years before all its houses were built. Those on the east side were built from 1788 to 1794, on the west from 1791 to 1797, on the north from 1794 to 1810 and the south from 1797 to 1802. Nevertheless it made a very pleasant square. *The Leeds Guide* of 1806 said of St. Paul's Square: 'though the houses are not equal to those of Park Place, they are all well built in the modern style. The area of the square is laid out with considerable taste, and in a few years will furnish a very agreeable promenade'.

The initial naming of Park Square as 'St. Paul's Square' was because the elegance and desirability of the square was considerably enhanced by the erection of St. Paul's Church in its south-east corner. This handsome classical church with a tower and cupola completed in 1793 was paid for by its minister, Reverend Miles Atkinson, on land given by Christopher Wilson, Bishop of Bristol. It was a proprietary church for the worthies of the Park Estate and had a vaulted crypt for burials.

Amongst the well-known people living in Park Square in 1809 were Edward Baines, who came from Preston and was the proprietor of *Leeds Mercury* and Thomas Bolland, Clerk to the Lieutenancy Meetings, Attorney and Notary Public. Sir Peter Fairbairn (see page 40) lived at 11 Park Square in 1839 before moving to his mansion on Clarendon Road.

The Park Square Plaque was sponsored by Simpson Curtis, Solicitors and unveiled by Mr. Anthony Blackmore, Senior Partner of Simpson Curtis, on 21st September 1989. It is at 45, Park Square, Leeds 1.

Fairbairn House

Originally known as Woodsley House, this monumental villa was built in 1840 for Sir Peter Fairbairn, the textile engineering magnate, and Mayor of Leeds 1858-59. Queen Victoria stayed here in 1858 when she came to open the Town Hall.

Peter Fairbairn was born in Kelso, Scotland in 1799. His parents moved to Newcastle, where, at eleven years of age, he was taken from school and apprenticed to the business of a millwright. He received part of his business training working for his eldest brother, William Fairbairn, in Manchester. In 1824 he became a partner in the firm of Houldsworth & Co., of the Anderton Foundry, Glasgow. In 1828 he moved to Leeds and started the business of machine maker, first producing machines for the woollen industry, then making improved machinery for preparing and spinning flax. For several years he was the principal supplier of machines to the Marshalls in Holbeck. During the Crimean War Fairbairn's company made machine tools for the production of armaments and munitions.

Fairbairn took an active interest in public affairs, and in 1836 was elected a town councillor. In 1854 he was elected alderman of the borough, and Mayor of Leeds 1858-59.

He built Woodsley House in Clarendon Road in 1840, designed by the Leeds-based architect, John Clark. It is built in red brick with stone Greek columns on the front. In the hall and at the foot of the lovely staircase are similar Corinthian columns to match those on the outside. The house was described as an unpretentious mansion, but full of elegance and comfort inside. There was a magnificent drawing room and the dining room was decorated in Italian style. An attractive hillside led up to it, and it stood in beautiful grounds, the back of the houses overlooked 'the hills and picturesque valleys of Kirkstall Vale'.

When Queen Victoria came to Leeds for the official opening of Leeds Town Hall on 6th September 1858, she and her entourage stayed the previous night at Woodsley House. During the splendid ceremony and in front of a brilliant assembly in the Town Hall, Queen Victoria conferred the title of Knight Bachelor on Peter Fairbairn.

Sir Peter, as he now was, died in Woodsley House in 1861. His son, who became Sir Andrew Fairbairn, lived in the house until 1870, but in 1865 the grounds of the house were put up for auction in forty-four plots varying in size from 3,600 to 900 square yards.

The Fairbairn House Plaque was sponsored by the University of Leeds and unveiled by Colonel Alan Roberts, Pro-Chancellor of the University of Leeds on 20th June 1991. It is at 71, Clarendon Road, Leeds 2.

Potternewton Mansion

This neat, neo-classical house, formerly Harehills Grove, was built c. 1817 for James Brown, woollen merchant. From 1861 to 1900 it was the home of the Jowitt family. It now belongs to Park Lane College.

The mansion is a reminder of the days when much of the land a couple of miles north of Leeds city centre was divided into large estates owned by wealthy woollen merchants and bankers. First known as Harehills Grove, it was built for James Brown, a notable Leeds woollen merchant, about 1817, and stood in a 750 acre estate, approximately the same area as Roundhay Park. Brown created a 30 acre park in front of his house.

The increase in the middle-class population of Leeds provided the stimulus to develop stylish residential estates. In the 1820s Earl Cowper began to develop his land, south of the Brown's estate, on the east side of Chapeltown Road with high-class houses in Cowper Street, Leopold Street and Spencer Place. In 1861 Robert Benson Jowitt, a woollen merchant and Leeds magistrate rented the mansion and its park.

In 1877 the Brown family decided to sell their large estate. Substantial parts were purchased by Sir James Kitson and the merchant E. Schunk, who built themselves mansions in small estates, and the Jowitts bought Harehills Grove and its park. The rest of the land, however, was sold in smaller plots which, due to the great pressure to house the working classes, became densely packed areas of terraced and back-to-back houses.

When the Jowitts moved from Harehills Grove to Tunbridge Wells in 1900, Leeds Corporation had the

foresight to buy the mansion and the 30 acres of mature gardens and parkland to create Potternewton Park. In 1906 the mansion was formally re-opened as a Museum and Picture Gallery. Its fine collection of stuffed birds was a popular attraction, as was its cafe.

In 1929 the mansion became the new home of the Leeds School for Cripples and Delicate Children (founded in 1904). After the second world war it was renamed simply as Potternewton Mansion School. On 10th November 1954 the Golden Jubilee Anniversary of the opening of the school was celebrated. The ceremony was attended by the Lady Mayoress, Mr. Kenneth Hudson, (grandson of Mrs Robert Hudson, who founded the Leeds Branch of the Invalid Children's Aid Society and was very closely involved with the School) and 400 guests. The school had places for over 100 children.

During the 1960s the mansion became an annexe of Park Lane College, and is its centre for Management Studies and Trade Union Studies.

The Potternewton Mansion Plaque was sponsored by Park Lane College and unveiled by Fabian Hamilton, MP on 1st October 1999. It is at Potternewton Mansion, Harehills Lane, Leeds 7.

The Old Grammar School

EDUCATION

In the centuries before the State provided a comprehensive system, education was for only the children of affluent families or for poor children who were fortunate enough to gain places at schools run by charitable foundations. In 1547 William Sheffield founded Leeds Grammar School 'to teach and freely instruct young scholars, youths and children'. This small school was re-endowed by the merchant John Harrison who in 1624 built a new school house for it close to St. John's Church.

The Grammar School taught mainly the sons of better off Leeds townspeople, and so in 1705 the Charity School (or Blue Coat School) was established in the former Leeds Workhouse giving a basic education to forty pauper girls and boys. Because the two schools educated only a handful of children, most better-off Leeds townspeople in the eighteenth and early nineteenth centuries turned to private schools and academies for the education of their children. Kemplay's Academy started in the early nineteenth century was the most famous of these.

But the need to give the mass of the population at least a basic education in reading, writing and arithmetic became more compelling as the Industrial Revolution progressed. In Leeds the first significant steps were taken with the establishment of Sunday Schools from the 1780s. The opening of the Royal Lancasterian School in 1811 and the National School in 1813, primary schools accommodating about 1000 pupils, run on the monitorial system by the religious denominations, provided for the first time a low cost education for large numbers of children.

Despite a great increase in the number of such schools, religious and voluntary organisations simply could not adequately provide for the rapidly growing numbers of children in Leeds. In 1870 Parliament required local authorities to meet the shortfall. As a result Leeds School Board was established in that year and began erecting Board Schools.

The further development of industry and commerce created a significant demand for secondary education and for education in key skills. Leeds College of Art founded in 1846 was one of the products of this demand, while towards the end of the century the Leeds School Board, in a bid to provide secondary education, set up the Leeds Central Higher Grade School.

Right into the Victorian period the education of girls beyond an elementary level was viewed as unimportant. Later in the nineteenth century, however, some individuals and organisations worked hard to redress the balance. One such prominent Leeds organisation was the Yorkshire Ladies' Council of Education.

Leeds Charity School

The chapel of Harrison's Almshouses, which formerly occupied this site, was converted for use by the Charity School in 1726. When the present building was erected in 1815, the institution clothed 80 poor girls in blue and trained them for domestic service. Founded 1705.

Concern about the lack of a school in Leeds for pauper children led to the establishment of the Charity School (sometimes called the Blue Coat School) in 1705, in the temporarily disused Leeds Workhouse building on Lady Lane. The school was financed by public subscription for the maintenance and education of forty poor children in the principles of the Church of England, and to teach them in reading writing and arithmetic, to qualify them for a trade. Ralph Thoresby noted that there was a pew against 'the north wall of the Parish Church for the master and mistress of the Charity School with forty poor boys and girls decently clad in blue'. When the Workhouse was reopened in 1726, the Charity School needed a new home and it 'was removed to the chapel in St. John's Hospital Yard, where one half was taught by Mr. John Lucas and the other half in a house adjoining to the old church yard, built and given by William Cookson'. The chapel had been built by John Harrison for the forty residents of the almshouses he had built next to St. John's Church around 1634.

The schools were reunited in 1750 in the chapel buildings, and at the same time the practice of housing and feeding the scholars was discontinued and the charity was limited to clothing and educating the children. By mid-century the school taught the three R's to seventy boys, and reading, writing and knitting to fifty girls, all in the 7 to 14 years age range. Boys were provided with a coat, waistcoat, breeches and cap of blue cloth, a pair of leather breeches, four shirts, two pairs of stockings and two pairs of shoes. Girls were given a gown and petticoat of blue cloth, a straw hat, a pair of leather stays ('which were to last the whole time they remained at school'), four shifts, two pairs of stockings, and two pairs of shoes.

The opening of the National and Lancasterian Schools in early nineteenth century Leeds reduced the need for the Charity School. In 1815 the chapel building was demolished and replaced by the present day school house (now Age Concern) where girls were trained to be household servants. The building ceased to be a school at the end of the nineteenth century, when the school moved to Chapeltown Road.

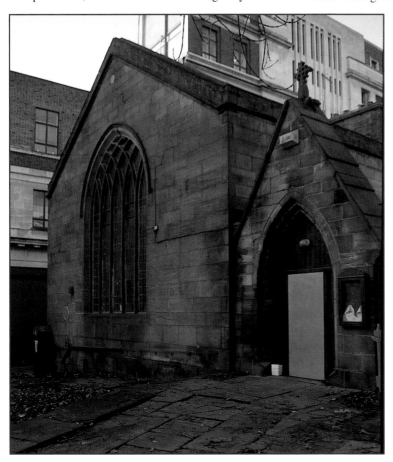

The Leeds Charity School Plaque was sponsored by Professor N. R. Rowell, Vice-President of Leeds Civic Trust, and unveiled by him on 30th October 1989. It is at Mark Lane, Leeds 2.

Kemplay's Acadamy

This fine house, built in 1720 for Matthew Wilson, is shown on John Cossins' Plan of Leeds in 1725. In 1817 Richard Kemplay purchased the property to house his 'Academy for Young Gentlemen'.

This building, which is now Nash's Tudor Fish Restaurant, occupies one of the most complete eighteenth century houses left in the city centre. The south side of the building was constructed for Matthew Wilson in 1720 and is clearly visible on Cossins' plan of 1726, and Buck's panorama of 1745. It apparently cost more than Matthew Wilson had anticipated, a fact noted by the historian Whitaker who claimed that the venture had led to Wilson's ruin. Despite these difficulties he did not dispose of the property until 1743, when a relative, Joshua Wilson of Pontefract, purchased the house and adjoining land.

The most notable owner of the house was Richard Kemplay who, in 1817, acquired the 'dwelling house with stable, greenhouse and other outbuildings'. Richard Kemplay was by this time a most respected member of the community, whose Academy was famed for its high standards. He realised the potential of the site and quickly constructed a large extension to the west of the mansion house. This provided accommodation for pupils who boarded at the school. The core curriculum consisted of English, Mathematics, Geography, Latin and Greek, though parents could pay extra should they wish their child to benefit from lessons in French, German and Drawing.

Kemplay believed in the publication of results. In 1828 Joseph Parkinson came top of the class as he made only four errors during the writing of twenty dictations.

Poor Charles Cockerham must have been mortified at his appalling performance ....288 mistakes!

Richard Kemplay died in 1830 aged 60. He was described as having a 'truly benevolent and philanthropic disposition'. The Academy continued to prosper under his son Christopher Kemplay, however, and in 1842 the opportunity arose for Christopher to purchase a share in the *Leeds Intelligencer*, a paper which he was to edit for over twenty-four years.

The Academy site was split in to two, the boarding quarters were converted into a synagogue, and the old mansion house became the home of the Victoria Club which was founded in 1877 and continued to 1960, when the members were devastated by the termination of their tenancy.

Nash's Tudor Fish Restaurant opened in December 1963. The advertising feature claimed that it bore 'as much resemblance to the traditional fish and chip shop as the Queen's Hotel does to a transport caff'.

The Kemplay's Academy Plaque was sponsored by Mr. Lawrence Bellhouse, proprietor of Nash's Tudor Fish Restaurant, and was unveiled by him, in May 1989. It is at Nash's Tudor Fish Restaurant, off New Briggate, Leeds 1

Leeds School Board

Leeds School Board erected this fine headquarters and examination centre, designed by architect George Corson, in 1878 - 81. First elected by the ratepayers of Leeds in 1870, the Board built sufficient schools to ensure that for the first time every child in Leeds received an elementary education.

In the late Georgian and early Victorian eras education for working-class children in England was provided by the remarkable efforts of voluntary organisations, the great majority of these were associated with church or chapel. The inadequacies of this provision prompted Forster's Education Act of 1870 which aimed to create a national system of elementary education. While the act encouraged the voluntary schools to expand, it decreed that State schools should be provided to fill in the gaps. These would be known as 'board schools' because they were to be provided by locally elected School Boards financed by local rates and government grants.

Leeds' first School Board was elected on 28 November 1870. A census of children showed that 48,787 should be attending school, but there was accommodation for only 27,329. The School Board's response was one of the great achievements of Victorian Leeds. By November 1878 no less than 31 large schools capable of accommodating 19,000 pupils had been erected in the borough at a cost of £177,000.

In 1876 the School Board decided to erect its own purpose-built offices on Calverley Street. The School Board Offices were the centre to which trainee teachers and children came for their examinations, and also the administrative centre, where the new schools were designed, and from where they were supplied with their equipment. The showpiece of the building was the Board Room with a gallery, 12 feet high walnut panelling, and shields and busts commemorating Board Chairmen and Leeds worthies. The examination room too was very impressive. Nave-like in appearance, it was forty-three feet high, with narrow aisles formed by the cast iron pillars supporting the arched ribs of the roof. It had standing room for 1000 people, and a gallery for 100 spectators.

The School Board Offices and the Municipal Buildings next door were both designed by the now highly admired George Corson (1829-1910), a Scottish architect who moved to Leeds in 1849. Under the cipher 'Crayon' he won the competition for the design of the Municipal Building and the School Board Offices in November 1876.

The Leeds School Board Plaque was sponsored by The Rushbond Group and unveiled by Councillor Graham Kirkland, Lord Mayor of Leeds, on 2nd October 1998. It is at Civic Court, Calverley Street, Leeds 1.

Leeds College of Art

Founded in 1846, by Leeds Mechanics' and Literary Institution, pioneered the teaching of practical art and design in England and USA. Henry Moore & Barbara Hepworth studied here. This building was erected for the college in 1903.

The provision of technical and adult education was an issue of increasing concern in the early nineteenth century. The Mechanics Institute founded in 1824 only attracted small classes, mainly from the middle classes. With the aid of Government finance in 1846, the Institute was able to establish the Leeds College of Art as a 'Government School of Design', and from this point Leeds became a centre of art education.

In 1852 the name was changed to the Leeds School of Practical Art. The 1858 *Guide to Leeds* noted: 'This important school, which is a branch of the Mechanic's Institute and Literary Society, and also connected with the Department of Science and Art, South Kensington, was established for the purpose of instructing young men who when either preparing for, or engaged in, art, industry or manufactures, required a more elaborate system of instruction than could otherwise be given. The results have shown that such an establishment is most useful.'

James Hole, Secretary of the Mechanics' Institute, had argued that if art instruction was to prosper in Leeds a large and commodious building must be erected, expressly adapted to give all classes general art instruction, and to workmen a practical knowledge of the essential art elements in their various trades. 'There are hundreds of working men, such as masons, builders, joiners, mechanics, carvers, house painters, upholsterers, cabinet makers etc. to whom a knowledge of drawing would be most useful.' The new Mechanics' Institute building on Cookridge Street which opened in 1868 provided this space.

In 1871 the headmaster of the school accepted the invitation to become the Director of Art for all the publicly provided schools in Massachusetts. Hence Leeds School of Art was the Alma Mater of art education in the U S A.

In 1903 the Leeds School of Art moved in to its own purpose-built premises in Vernon Street on which the plaque is displayed; the architects were Francis William Bedford and Sydney Decimus Kitson.

In 1907 the School was taken over by Leeds City Council.

Henry Moore attended the School for two years from September 1919 following his recovery from the effects of gas shells whilst serving in the British Army at Cambrai in the summer of 1917. He was then awarded a Royal Exhibition Scholarship to study at the Royal College of Art and in September 1921 he moved to London. Barbara Hepworth joined the School in 1920, where she met Henry Moore. Their lifelong friendship and reciprocal influence was an important factor in the parallel development of their careers.

The Leeds College of Art Plaque was sponsored by the Henry Moore Foundation and unveiled by Sir Alan Bowness, former Director of the Henry Moore Foundation, former Director of the Tate Gallery and son-in-law of Barbara Hepworth on 5th March 1996. It is at Leeds College of Art, Vernon Street, Leeds 2.

Central Higher Grade School

This imposing school was erected by Leeds School Board as the town's first local authority secondary school. Renamed City of Leeds School in 1928, it merged with Thoresby High School in 1972, and moved to a new site in 1994. Opened 1889.

Mute and Blind children and scholars taking Cookery Instruction, Physical Training etc; 1st floor 752 boys; 2nd floor 752 girls; 3rd floor 454 Science and Art students.

One of the school's unusual features was its flat roof, which was used as an extra playground.

During the First World War the school admitted Belgian boys who came to Leeds as refugees, and also taught members of the Serbian Army to speak English. During World War Two pupils and teachers were evacuated to Lincoln, and the school became the Government Headquarters for the Ministry of Food.

It provided education for boys until 1972 when it merged with Thoresby High School for girls.

The school closed in December 1993, 104 years after its opening, and moved to its present site in Woodhouse. Leeds City Council opened the converted building to the public in 1995 as its pioneering one-stop shop, offering a wide range of Council services and advice to around 1,200 people a day.

The Central Higher Grade School Plaque was sponsored by Leeds City Council and unveiled by Councillor Suzi Armitage, Chair of the Community Benefits and Rights Committee of Leeds City Council, on 16th September 1997. It is at 2 Great George Street, Leeds 1.

The Central Higher Grade School building on Woodhouse Lane has been a landmark in the City of Leeds for over one hundred years. The renovated building contains many original features of the school such as the tiled staircase, the chalkboard and the school clock. A memorial to the Leeds' teachers who were killed in the First World War, which formerly hung in the Council's Education Department on Calverley Street, is now displayed in this building.

Until the late 1880s Leeds School Board provided only elementary education for Leeds children and secondary education remained essentially the preserve of the middle and upper classes who sent their children to private schools. In its first attempt to redress this imbalance, in 1885 the Board opened the Central Higher Grade School in temporary accommodation. In November 1889 the school moved into the magnificent building familiar to us today, erected at a cost of £48,000.

Incredibly, according to its first prospectus, it accommodated 2,500 pupils: Ground floor 542 Deaf,

The Yorkshire Ladies' Council of Education

The Yorkshire Ladies' Council of Education was founded in 1876 to promote the education of girls and women and occupied this building between 1928 - 1988. It served as an administrative centre for Council activities and housed The Yorkshire Ladies' Secretarial College.

The lack of formal education for young women and girls was a cause of increasing concern in the middle of the nineteenth century. On 8th March 1865 a Grace was passed by the Cambridge Senate admitting girls to the Local Examinations. At the end of 1865 the first Cambridge Examination for girls took place in Sheffield, and five of the six candidates passed. In response to a request made by the West Riding Board of Education a meeting was held at 'Claremont', 23, Clarendon Road, Leeds, the home of Dr. and Mrs John Heaton, on 8th September 1866. Miss Emily Davies, who helped in the forming of and became the first Mistress of Girton College, spoke at this meeting and it was decided to support the Cambridge Local Examinations. A small Ladies' Committee was formed under the presidency of Mrs. Heaton.

During the next ten years the ladies on this committee were joined by others who actively promoted the higher education of women on 'The Leeds Ladies' Educational Association', (which was dissolved in April 1982) and 'The Ladies' Honorary Council of the Yorkshire Board of Education', which became 'The Yorkshire Ladies' Council of Education' in August 1876.

Both the Council and the Association were actively considering the establishment of a high-class girls'

school in Leeds, and in 1875 they set up a joint committee comprising six members from each group with their presidents and honorary secretaries. The Leeds Girls' High School Company was formed with the Vicar of Leeds, the Rev. John Gott as President; Mrs. Frances Lupton, Vice President; two honorary secretaries, Mrs. R. W. Eddison and Mrs. J. D. Heaton; and Mr. J. M. Ford as the company's solicitor. The High School was opened at St. James' Lodge, Woodhouse Lane, in September 1876.

There are many notable achievements connected with the Council, including the opening of the Yorkshire Ladies' Secretarial School at 7, Cookridge Street in 1918, and the establishment of the Personal Service and Citizens' Advice Bureau in 1938, which together with the Old People's Welfare (1941) led to the formation of the Leeds Council of Social Service which became independent in 1944.

The Yorkshire Ladies' Council of Education Plaque was sponsored by Mr. and Mrs Peter Hartley, Hillards Charitable Trust and unveiled by The Lady Grimthorpe D.C.V.O. Past President of Yorkshire Ladies Council of Education on 2nd March 1995. It is at 18, Blenheim Terrace, Leeds 2

HEALTH &
POOR RELIEF

Adequate income and savings to keep the wolf from the door, good healthcare, and death with dignity must have been the desire of most Leeds people for centuries. For the majority of Leeds people these aspirations were difficult to fulfil before the twentieth century, but during the eighteenth and nineteenth centuries considerable, if not always successful efforts, were made to bring greater comfort and security to the poorer members of the community.

In 1768 the General Infirmary at Leeds was founded to provide free medical treatment primarily for the working classes of Leeds. It soon gained a national reputation as did its senior surgeon and leading light William Hey. Its first purpose-built premises in Infirmary Street were superseded in 1869 by the impressive new building in Great George Street familiar to us today. The rapidly growing town required many surgeons and doctors and in 1813 the Leeds School of Medicine was founded, one of the first in the country.

Inevitably, due to economic fluctuations and family upheavals Leeds had many social casualties who particularly through unemployment or infirmity could not support themselves. In the 1860s the old Leeds Workhouse in Lady Lane was replaced by the much larger and grander Leeds Union Workhouse in Beckett Street. It had its own infirmary to cater for the needs of the pauper inmates.

In the days before the Welfare State all classes of Leeds society looked for ways of saving people from destitution and the humiliation of the workhouse. The working classes set up friendly societies to provide support for fellow workers in hard times, while the middle classes set up benevolent societies and organisations to encourage the habit of thrift amongst the working classes. Perhaps the country's most famous Savings Bank was the Yorkshire Penny Bank, today known as the Yorkshire Bank, which was founded in Leeds in 1856.

The huge increase in the population of Leeds in the early nineteenth century put great pressure on housing, the provision of clean water and good sanitation. It also made the prospect of a dignified repose after death less possible. The town's grave yards almost literally overflowed with the bodies of the dead. The Town Council solved the problem in 1845 when it opened the country's first municipal cemetery.

Leeds Infirmary

The General Infirmary moved here from Infirmary Street in 1869. The building, designed by George Gilbert Scott, incorporated ideas from Florence Nightingale. The plan placed it in the foremost rank of European hospitals.

In England at the beginning of the eighteenth century, apart from a few workhouse infirmaries, there was no public accommodation available for treating the poor who were ill or injured, except for the two chartered hospitals in London - St Bartholomew's and St. Thomas's.

The voluntary hospital movement began in London with the Westminster Hospital in 1720. This was followed by provincial hospitals at Winchester (1736), Bristol (1736), York (1740) and others so that by 1800 there were 38 general hospitals in the provinces, including the General Infirmary in Leeds which was founded in 1767.

The Infirmary was established in Mr. Andrew Wilson's house in Kirkgate, and the first in-patients were admitted on 2nd October 1767. It was funded entirely by voluntary subscriptions and donations, treated the poor - usually without charge - and was intended to be a ' General' Infirmary, not to be limited to patients from Leeds. The provision of the Infirmary showed a measure of social responsibility on the part of the

middle and upper classes, and also the will to get their sick and injured employees back to work, and off the poor rates. The house in Kirkgate was regarded as only temporary, and on 1st March 1771 the first patients were admitted to the purpose-built premises in Infirmary Street designed by John Carr. It had 27 beds for in-patients. Three extensions brought the number of beds to 108 by 1792.

In 1859 it was decided that the 150 beds then available were too few. This present site was purchased in 1862 and Mr (later Sir) George Gilbert Scott was appointed architect. Miss Florence Nightingale gave advice on many details of the building, and considered that all wards must always be under the supervision of a nurse, and that the maximum number of patients in a ward should be 32. The first patient was admitted into the new building on 22nd May 1869. The Infirmary has been extended by the opening of additional wards and operating theatres, the Brotherton Wing in 1940 being the last before the National Health Service Act was passed in November 1946 The Leeds General Infirmary now has 1334 beds.

The Leeds Infirmary Plaque was sponsored by the Medical Faculty of the General Infirmary at Leeds and unveiled by Professor N. R. Rowell MD, FRCP, Vice President of Leeds Civic Trust, on 12th March 1990. It is at Leeds General Infirmary, Great George Street, Leeds 1.

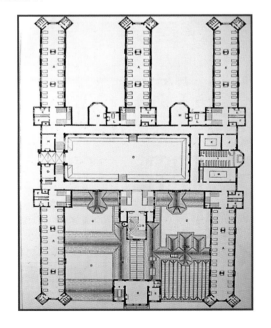

William Hey's House

This impressive Georgian townhouse, erected between 1794 and 1795, was designed by architect Thomas Johnson and built for William Hey (1736-1819) one of the founders and later Chief Surgeon of Leeds General Infirmary. For 50 years Hey was in in the front rank of British surgeons.

William Hey was born in Pudsey in 1736, the third son of Richard and Mary Hey. Richard was a drysalter and sold oils and chemicals used by clothiers in the Aire Valley. He was a very pious man who had great influence over his son, not only in religious matters. Mary was the daughter of Jacob Simpson, apothecary-surgeon, who practised in the Upper Headrow, Leeds. They married in 1730 when Mary was 28, and had five sons and three daughters.

When William was three years old his dress caught fire and he was nearly burnt to death. When he was four he lost the sight of his right eye as a result of playing with a penknife. In later life he damaged a leg so badly that he could only walk with the aid of a crutch.

William Hey went to school at Heath near Wakefield where he acquired a taste for natural philosophy and learned modern languages. He became proficient in French which was useful to him later as at that time France led in medical research. He wanted to go to sea, but submitted to his parents wishes that he study medicine in the hope that he might become a naval surgeon. From 1750 to 1757 he was apprenticed to William Dawson, apothecary-surgeon in Kirkgate, then spent two years gaining experience in London, 'walking the wards' of a hospital. In 1759 William set up in practice at the Slip-Inn Yard (now the Pack Horse Yard) Briggate. He married Alice Banks on 30th July 1761, daughter of Robert Banks, the Squire of Giggleswick. They had 14 children, only 5 of them are thought to have survived infancy.

In 1767 he was elected surgeon to the newly founded General Infirmary at Leeds, where he founded a medical society, and gave courses on anatomy. Bodies of executed criminals were used for dissection and anatomical demonstration in the Infirmary. On 7th October 1812 William Hey resigned his office of Surgeon to the Infirmary. He had served the institution for more than 45 years, 39 years as senior surgeon. For more than 50 years he was in the front rank of British surgeons in this pre-antiseptic period, and in 1775 was elected a Fellow of the Royal Society. He also played his part in the public life of Leeds, being elected Common Councilman in 1781, Alderman in 1786 and Mayor of Leeds in 1787 and 1801. Hey was the first president of a Philosophical and Literary Society formed in 1783. When it was re-established in 1818 he presided over its first meeting. He was still visiting patients two weeks before he died on 23rd March 1819, aged eighty-three.

The William Hey's House Plaque was sponsored by Leeds Law Society and erected in March 1990. It is at Albion Place, Leeds 1.

Leeds School of Medicine

This institution, founded in 1831, was one of the first provincial medical schools in England. The move here from Park Street in 1894 provided the school with its second purpose-built premises which were designed by architect W. H. Thorp and erected between 1891 and 1894.

An outline of the education and training of an apothecary-surgeon in the late eighteenth century as experienced by William Hey is set out on page 51. The Apothecaries Act of 1815 and the laying down of detailed regulations by the Court of Examiners of the Worshipful Society of Apothecaries helped to formalise the training required, but it was still widely felt that surgeons were not adequately carrying out their obligation to instruct their pupils. In 1826 Charles Turner Thackrah established a private school of anatomy at 9 South Parade, but his establishment was not recognised by the Court of Examiners of the Royal College of Surgeons. In 1831 an enthusiastic group of Leeds medical men including Adam Hunter, James Williamson, Samuel Smith, William Hey III, Thomas Pridgin Teal, and Joseph Prince Garlick invited Thackrah to join them in establishing the Leeds School of Medicine at Leeds Public Dispensary in North Street. The school proved a success, and moved to 1 East Parade in 1834. In this building experiments were conducted in 1846-47 on the use of ether as an anaesthetic.

In 1865 the school moved again, to purpose-built

premises designed by George Corson in Park Street, close to the site where the new infirmary was being built. The Park Street school accommodated an annual intake of 40 students, by 1889 increasing pressure for more places required a move to larger premises. Whilst

THORESBY PLACE

at Park Place, Thomas Scattergood was associated with the institution and he helped to achieve its amalgamation with the Yorkshire College which had been founded in 1874. In 1884 it became the Faculty of Medicine at the Yorkshire College with Scattergood as its first Dean.

In 1894 the new Medical School building at Thoresby Place was opened, designed to accommodate 400 students - an annual intake of 80 for a five year course. William H. Thorpe, who designed Leeds Art Gallery, was its architect. From May 1894 the new department of physiology was in use. In October 1894 the building was officially opened by their Royal Highnesses, the Duke and Duchess of York (later King George V and Queen Mary). The entrance hall of the new building is particularly striking. It is hexagonal and lined with Burmantofts faience tiles, decorated with the arms of the Royal College of Physicians and Surgeons, the Victoria University of Manchester (of which Yorkshire College was part) and the Faculty of Medicine.

The Leeds School of Medicine Plaque was sponsored by the Faculty of Medicine, University of Leeds, and unveiled by Professor M. S. Losowsky, Dean of the Faculty of Medicine and Professor of Medicine, The University of Leeds, on 3rd April 1990. It is at Thoresby Place, Leeds 1.

1 EAST PARADE

Leeds Union Workhouse

Leeds Union Workhouse, designed by architects Perkin & Backhouse, opened in 1861 at a cost of £32,000 to accommodate 800 paupers. In 1944 it became part of St James's Hospital, and in 1995-97 it was splendidly refurbished as the Thackray Medical Museum.

The Union Workhouse opened in 1861 and its infirmary eventually became St. James's Hospital. As a result many Leeds people associated treatment at St. James's with the social stigma of poverty and dependence. People's hearts must have sunk as they passed through the portals of the workhouse for, despite its external grandeur, it was an admission that they had reached the utmost levels of destitution and despair. Happily today, people can visit the building for an extremely enjoyable and stimulating experience in its new guise as the Thackray Medical Museum.

Sympathy for the poor and disadvantaged, and willingness to contribute to their well being seems always to have been dogged by doubts about the best way to provide help without exacerbating the problem. In the 1830s there was strong pressure in national government circles for the reform of the Poor Law, to reduce the form of relief which enabled the poor to live in their own homes. This was paid according to family size and as a subsidy to low wages, and was believed to encourage idleness and population growth and to distort the free operation of the labour market. The Poor Law Amendment Act of 1834 aimed to reduce out-door relief and to restrict benefits to those whose need was so desperate that they were willing to enter the workhouse. This was unacceptable to the people of Leeds. It was clearly cheaper to support a man and his family in his own home and in periods of high unemployment it seemed physically impractical to do anything else. Moreover, families were terrified of entering the workhouse where they were separated. In 1843 an inspection of the Leeds Workhouse in Lady Lane showed it to be overcrowded, with young and old, men and women, infirm and able thrown together; altogether discreditable to a civilised society. In 1844 Leeds made a partial implementation of the 1834 Act by establishing a Board of Guardians. They purchased land in Beckett Street and built the Moral and Industrial Training School, which opened in 1848 to maintain and educate orphans and a few children of the deserving poor. The 499 children accommodated spent half their time on school work and half on industrial training. In 1850 it was decided to build a new workhouse, the foundation stone was laid on 5th April 1858 alongside the Moral and Industrial School. A workhouse chapel was erected between the two buildings. The new workhouse building provided accommodation for 810 paupers, 360 males and 450 females.

The Leeds Union Workhouse Plaque was sponsored by Thackray Medical Museum and unveiled by Mr. Paul Thackray, the founder of the Thackray Medical Museum, on 11th February 1998. It is at the Thackray Medical Museum, Beckett Street, Leeds 9.

Yorkshire Penny Bank

This famous bank, later known as Yorkshire Bank, was founded at Leeds in 1856. These flamboyant premises, designed by G. B. Bulmer, were opened in 1894. The first purpose-built Leeds General Infirmary (1771) formerly stood on this site.

The Yorkshire Penny Bank was one of the most successful 'self-help' savings institutions established in England in the mid-nineteenth century. Apart from providing a most useful institution encouraging the Victorian working classes to save, it also made a major contribution to the architectural quality of Leeds city centre by erecting its Infirmary Street building in lavish style. This fine building, designed by G.B. Bulmer of the firm of Messrs Perkin and Bulmer, Architects, Leeds, in 1894, occupies the site of the first purpose-built General Infirmary at Leeds erected in 1771. The Infirmary was founded in 1768 and had its first premises in the Rotation Office Yard off Kirkgate. The Infirmary moved to Great George Street in 1869.

The Yorkshire Penny Bank was founded by Colonel Edward Akroyd, one of Halifax's foremost woollen and worsted manufacturers. He is said to have been inspired in this project by the sermons of the Christian Socialist, Reverend Charles Kingsley (of *The Water Babies* fame). In May 1856 Akroyd circulated a pamphlet amongst the nobility and wealthy gentry of the county advocating the establishment of a Penny Savings Bank. This was followed by a meeting in Leeds Philosophical Hall on 17th November 1856. Essentially well to do patrons were needed to provide a fund of money for the stability of the bank. Its first permanent central office was established in 1858 at 2, East Parade, Leeds. The first branches were often simply rooms in a school hall hired for one evening each week. Colonel Akroyd said that in setting up the bank he aimed for a convenient and safe 'reservoir' into which the worker 'could squeeze drop by drop from his

scanty earnings all that he could spare above the minimum needed to keep his family.' The bank flourished and on 25th August 1894 the *Yorkshire Weekly Post* described the opening of the new premises: 'The palatial structure in which the business of the Yorkshire Penny Bank is now carried on was formally opened on Friday by the Duke of Devonshire in the presence of a company that was thoroughly representative of the banking, commercial and industrial interests of the County. The fine Gothic edifice, noble in its proportions and graceful in its external and internal adornments has been well described as one of the handsomest buildings in Leeds, and this opinion was corroborated yesterday by the large crowds that gathered in Infirmary Street and Toronto Street and by those who followed the Duke and Duchess of Devonshire in their inspection of the interior arrangements of the building.'

The Yorkshire Penny Bank Plaque was sponsored by Yorkshire Bank plc and unveiled by Mr. David Mortimer, Controller (Marketing) Yorkshire Bank, on 1st February 1990. It is at the Yorkshire Bank plc, Infirmary Street, Leeds 1.

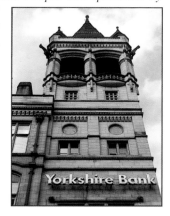

Leeds Burial Ground

Huge population growth led Leeds Town Council to pioneer the English municipal cemetery here at Beckett Street. When it opened in 1845, Anglicans and Dissenters had their own chapels and halves of the cemetery. The 27,000 graves, including many 'guinea graves' contain 180,000 interments

One of the great problems which faced Victorian cities was how to accommodate their dead. Rapidly growing populations and high death rates meant that existing churchyards and burial grounds could not cope. More affluent inhabitants established joint stock companies to provide private cemeteries such as Highgate in London and Undercliffe in Bradford. In Leeds the General Cemetery Company opened its cemetery at St. George's Field (now surrounded by Leeds University) in 1835.

Scandal arose in Leeds in the early 1840s when it was discovered that in Leeds Parish Church burial ground opposite the church it was only possible to bury bodies in family graves by smashing the coffins already in plots. The grave diggers also had to dig out coffins and hide them behind the vestry while new interments were taking place, and then put the coffins back later. The churchyard was so full of bodies that when it rained bones could be seen sticking out of the ground.

Beckett Street Cemetery was founded, together with Hunslet Cemetery, by an Act of Parliament secured by Leeds Town Council in 1842. It was a pioneering venture. It is believed that no town council had previously attempted to establish a cemetery with money raised by rates.

Beckett Street Cemetery - then known as Leeds Burial Ground - was opened in 1845 on a 16 acre site among the fields and brick kilns of Burmantofts. In the early days sheep grazed the cemetery to control the grass.

The cholera epidemic of 1849 emphasised the need for the cemetery, when 1,100 of the 1,600 Leeds victims were buried here. In 1849 the Moral and Industrial Training School was opened nearby; followed by the new workhouse. Many of the paupers from the workhouse were buried in the cemetery in the unmarked graves which fill so much of the area.

Another pioneering measure was the concept of the 'inscription or guinea grave', introduced in the 1880s. Although these graves with their simple headstones are now associated in many peoples' minds with poverty, they were once welcomed by those who could not afford a private plot and memorial but wanted to avoid the shame of lying uncommemorated in a common grave.

Although the cemetery is not officially closed, there are very few interments today, and these only in family graves.

The Leeds Burial Ground Plaque was sponsored by Mr. and Mrs. David Kaye, publishers of the Funeral Services Journal, and unveiled on 11th September 1998 by Mrs. Sylvia Barnard, founder of the Friends of Beckett Street Cemetery and author of 'To Prove I'm Not Forgot', which traces the history of the cemetery. It is opposite St. James's Hospital, Beckett Street, Leeds 9.

SOME OF THE GUINEA GRAVES

BRUNSWICK CHAPEL, LEEDS. N.W.

RELIGION

For centuries the Anglican Church held sway in Leeds, its domination highly visible in the grandeur of the Parish Church and St John's Church, New Briggate, and latterly Holy Trinity, Boar Lane. Nonconformity and Dissent began to make a significant mark from the mid-seventeenth century with the Dissenters opening the first Mill Hill Chapel in 1674 and Call Lane Chapel in 1691. In the seventeenth century non-Anglicans were a very much disapproved of minority. The Quakers, who built their first chapel down by the river in Water Lane in 1699, were hated almost as much as the few Catholics in the town. Dissent, nevertheless, found significant support amongst the merchant class, Ralph Thoresby for many years being a prominent worshipper at Mill Hill Chapel.

The rise in Nonconformity, especially Methodism, which accompanied the Industrial Revolution and the growth of the large urban working class, had a dramatic impact in Leeds. Since many merchants and mill owners were attracted to Nonconformity, in the early nineteenth century it was the financial contributions of both the rich and poor that built literally dozens of chapels in Leeds, including Brunswick Chapel, Oxford Place Chapel, South Parade Baptist Chapel and many more.

While a few proprietary Anglican churches were built, the only significant Anglican response to the spiritual needs of the rapidly growing masses was the building of the three Million Act churches, St Mary's, St Mark's and Christ Church, in working-class areas in the 1820s. When Dr Hook became Vicar of Leeds in 1837 he found Methodism the 'established religion' of Leeds. He immediately set about a campaign to revitalise Anglicanism in the parish, the result being the building of many new churches and church schools, and the establishment of the Church Institute.

The Victorian era was the great age of church and chapel building in Leeds, but is also brought new dimensions. The great influx of Irish immigrants and changes in civil attitudes gave a considerable fillip to Roman Catholicism, producing St Anne's Cathedral and Mount St Mary's Church. The arrival too of many Jewish immigrants from eastern Europe produced the large Jewish community in the Leylands, alongside North Street, whose needs were met by the establishment of the town's first synagogue.

Mill Hill Chapel

This elegant Gothic building, designed by Bowman and Crowther in 1848, replaced the original 17th century chapel. Its congregation - formerly Presbyterian, now Unitarian - dates from 1672. Joseph Priestley, LL.D., F.R.S., discoverer of oxygen, was minister here 1767-1773.

The years following the restoration of Charles the Second were anxious ones for those religious groups known as the Dissenters or Nonconformists. A series of repressive Acts of Parliament aided the widespread persecution of their brethren, and it was not until the Declaration of Indulgence in 1672 that they dared to come out into the open, to take up Royal licences to establish public places of worship. The Presbyterians were quick off the mark and by 1674 Mill Hill Chapel opened its doors to worshippers. Thoresby described it as the finest meeting house in the North of England. The cost of £400 was raised by propriety shares. With the addition of galleries in the eighteenth century it could seat 700 people.

The initial fervour for the older type of Nonconformism appears to have waned as the eighteenth century progressed and many of the rich merchants were lured back to Anglicanism. Further competition came from the Methodists who eventually established the 'Leeds Circuit'. Clearly an active, articulate, intelligent individual was required to revive the fortunes of Mill

Hill Chapel. In 1767 the trustees appointed Joseph Priestley. He wrote with great affection of the 'liberal friendly and harmonious congregation' with whom he was to share six 'very happy' years. When he moved to Leeds his house near the chapel was not ready, so temporarily he had to live in lodgings adjoining a brewery. A scientist of some note, he was quickly drawn into the brewhouse where, he recalled 'I at first amused myself with making experiments on the fixed air which I found ready made in the process of fermentation.' His experiments eventually led to the recognition of certain gases. During his stay in Leeds he published over thirty works, founded the Leeds Library (England's oldest surviving public subscription library) and became actively involved in supporting Leeds Infirmary. The birth of two sons placed a strain on the family budget and he was forced to move to a more lucrative position.

The first half of the nineteenth century saw the revival of the fortunes of the chapel. Many of the members of the congregation were successful business men who, after contemplating the restoration of the old building, decided that it was unsuitable for modern Unitarian worship. A fine new Gothic chapel, designed by Bowman and Crowther, was opened on December 27th, 1848, at a cost of over £7300. It remains one of the finest buildings in the City of Leeds.

The Mill Hill Chapel and Joseph Priestley Plaque was sponsored by Leeds & Holbeck Building Society and unveiled by Mrs Eila Forrester, President of the General Assembly of Victorian and Free Christian Churches on 28 March 1991. It is at the corner of Park Row and City Square, Leeds 1.

The Church Institute

Erected between 1866 and 1868 this was the power house behind the advancement of religious and secular education on the principles of the Church of England in Leeds, and a home for a host of Church organisations. The British Deaf Association was founded here on 24th July 1890.

The Leeds Church Institute was inaugurated on 17th January 1857, at the instigation of Dr. Walter Farquhar Hook. The objective of the Institute was 'to unite Churchmen in an endeavour to extend religious and secular knowledge consistently with the principles of the Church of England, by means of Lectures, a Library and Reading Room, and classes for religious and general instruction, and to promote the efficiency of Church Sunday Schools'. Its first home was in Bond Street in premises which had formerly been the Academy of Arts where it soon had a library of 1,500 books and a programme of fortnightly lectures. In 1859 the Institute moved to a spacious and convenient building in East Parade

In 1861 the Church Institute added 'and Sunday School Association' to its title, and sought larger premises.

Mr. Hey, one of the Vice Presidents, offered a site in Albion Place on advantageous terms. This being 'central, accessible and retired' was gratefully accepted. Plans for the new building were gratuitously drawn up and an appeal made for the building costs. On 29th October 1866 the foundation stone of the new building was laid by the Archbishop of Canterbury, and it was opened by the Bishop of Ripon on 16th June 1868.

The central organisation often acted as a pioneer, and much of the work originated by the Institute was devolved to the parishes.

In 1876 it added to its objects 'to maintain the interests of Church Day Schools' and later its facilities were extended to day school teachers.

The premises provided permanent accommodation for many Church organisations, and housed a unique accumulated store of knowledge on Church matters. It also provided a large lecture room and rooms for the meetings of almost every Society and Organisation connected with the Church and Church work.

On 24th July 1890 a Congress attended chiefly by deaf and dumb persons from the principal cities and towns of the United Kingdom was opened at the Institute. The Rev. W. B. Sleight of Northampton presided. The purpose was the formation of the National Deaf and Dumb Association with the objectives of protecting and promoting the interests of the deaf and dumb in education and in society.

In 1981 the Institute Library moved to Bond Street and the dilapidated Church Institute building was closed. It is now renovated as shops and offices. In 1994 the Institute moved to a large modern suite of rooms above Kirkgate Market and in 1999 moved again to New Market Street.

The Church Institute Plaque was sponsored by The British Deaf Association and erected in 1991. It is at Albion Place, Leeds 1.

First Leeds Synagogue

This plaque was erected to commemorate the 150th anniversary of the opening of the first Leeds synagogue in 1846 in a converted house near this site in Back Rockingham Street.

Although there is evidence of Jews living in Leeds a century earlier, it seems that it was only in the 1830s that there were sufficient numbers to make up a viable community. In 1840 the Jewish community held divine service in a small room in Bridge Street. This room was little better than a loft, and access was gained by means of a ladder.

Although there was only a slow growth in numbers it was evidently felt that there was a need for a proper synagogue to be established. For this purpose, on the initiative of Gabriel Davis, a house was purchased in Back Rockingham Street. After conversion this was opened for worship in 1846.

Gabriel Davis came to Leeds in 1817 and later set up as an optician and optical instrument maker at 24, Boar Lane. He became the first president of the synagogue and its first marriage secretary. There were seventeen weddings in the Back Rockingham Street synagogue during its fourteen years existence. The last one was between Samuel Manham and Rachel Friedman on 23rd May 1860. In a newspaper interview in 1918 Samuel Manham said 'I came to Leeds from Russia in 1852 and I was a fugitive from Russian Militiamen. I was on my way to America, via Hull and Liverpool, when someone in Hull persuaded me to go to Leeds. I took my chance here and have never regretted it. There were not more than a score of Jews in Leeds when I came and most of them lived in a lodging house at the bottom of Templar Street....... Later on men came with their wives from Russia, but the early ones were single who either made wives of Jewesses in this country or sent back to Russia for them. In my case I had a friend who sent to Russia for his sister and I married her.'

The country-wide religious census in 1851 gives a further indication of the size of the Leeds Jewish community. On Shabbat on 29th March 1851 there were 18 seat holders, the synagogue had 70 seats. There were 35 worshippers at morning service, the average number that normally attended, and at the mincha service that afternoon there was a congregation of 16. Ten children attended the Hebrew day school. From these small beginnings the vibrant Jewish community in Leeds has developed to be the third largest in Britain.

Back Rockingham Street and all the houses were cleared, and the area is included in the site of the Merrion Centre, which was opened in 1964.

The First Leeds Synagogue Plaque was sponsored by Mr. Edward Ziff, Town Centre Securities, and unveiled by the Lord Mayor of Leeds, Councillor Malcolm Bedford on 8th December 1996. It is in the Merrion Centre, Leeds 2.

THE BACK ROCKINGHAM STREET SYNAGOGUE WAS REPLACED BY THE GREAT SYNAGOGUE IN BELGRAVE STREET, SHOWN HERE AND ABOVE, OPENED IN 1878.

The Great Synagogue

In 1860 the first purpose-built synagogue in Yorkshire since the expulsion of the Jews from England in 1290 was erected here. Until 1983 it served the Jewish community which had settled in the Leylands (between North Street and Regent Street) in the 19th century.

THE WINDOWS IN THE GREAT SYNAGOGUE WERE RE-LOCATED IN THE NEW BUILDING IN SHADWELL LANE, LEEDS 17

In 1860 when the Back Rockingham Street synagogue became too small for its membership the congregation commissioned a new building from the architects Perkins and Backhouse. The new synagogue in Belgrave Street was formally opened in August 1861. This was the first purpose-built synagogue in Leeds, and probably the first one in Yorkshire since the expulsion of the Jewish community in the reign of Edward I in 1290.

This new building was described in McCorquodale's *Directory of Leeds 1876:* ' Its style is Byzantine and the internal fittings are very chaste, but the ark is a remarkably beautiful piece of workmanship.' It had accommodation for 400.

Further additions were made to the building. After a disastrous fire, in which all its records were destroyed, a completely new edifice was erected on the site and opened in September 1878. This new synagogue, which became known as The Great Synagogue, had the appearance of a large Nonconformist chapel. It continued in use for worship from its opening in 1878 to 1983.

In March 1881 the Tsar Alexander II of Russia was assassinated by revolutionaries.   In the resulting atmosphere of hostility and suspicion the anti-Jewish 'May Laws' were passed, and life became intolerable for the five million Jews living in Russia. Some two million Jews left Russia between 1881 and 1914, mostly going to America. During that time the Jewish population of Leeds rose from under 1,000 to nearly 20,000.

The new immigrants settled near to their fellow Jews in the Leylands, a compact area of shops, businesses and back-to-back houses on the northern edge of the city. It was soon overcrowded. Almost the whole of this area has been demolished and rebuilt.

The site on which the Great Synagogue stood is now occupied by an office block adjacent to Belgrave House, the Registry Office.

The Great Synagogue Plaque was sponsored by the United Hebrew Congregation and unveiled by Rabbi Dr. Solomon Brown on 3rd February 1991. It is at Belgrave Street, Leeds 2.

St. Aidan's Church

Built in 1894 to the designs of R J Johnson and A Crawford-Hick in the Italian Romanesque style. The eastern apse is adorned with fine mosaics depicting scenes from the life of St Aidan by Sir Frank Brangwyn.

When the building of this church, on a site donated by Lord Cowper, was being discussed, Dr. Jayne, the Vicar of Leeds, suggested that it should be planned in the form of a basilica. Three architects were invited to submit designs, and that of Robert James Johnson was selected. Johnson had been trained in Sir Gilbert Scott's office and established his practice in Newcastle in 1862. He built several churches in Tyneside, including Gosforth, Mitford, Stannington, Wylam and Newcastle. Sadly, Johnson died within a year of the acceptance of his design, and the work was completed by his successor A. Crawford-Hick.

The church is 188 ft long by 67 ft wide across the nave and aisles. The interior is entered through a small porch under the tower, which leads with dramatic suddenness into the vast space covered with a darkened timber vaulted roof. It has magnificent stone columns, coloured marbles and gilded metal-work on the pulpit with its domed canopy, and a monumental font in the apsidal baptistry at the west end of the church. Mexican onyx, red jasper, Irish green and Belgian blue marbles, pink alabaster and gold mosaics are reminders that although such colours and marbles have a long tradition of use in Italian churches, the opulent Edwardian age was about to open when St. Aidan's was consecrated in 1894.

The interior was completed in 1916 by the unveiling of Frank Brangwyn's wonderful mosaics. The principal one gloriously fills almost one thousand square feet behind the high altar, and illustrates the life of St. Aidan.

Frank Brangwyn (1867-1956) was the first British artist to achieve world wide recognition in his own lifetime. He brought a new dimension to British art with his compositions of vivid colours influenced by the grand manner of the Venetian decorators. His commissions ranged from the Uffizi Gallery in Florence and the Rockefeller Centre in New York to the House of Lords. His last is in Swansea Guildhall.

The initial commission was arranged by R. H. Kitson, who offered to pay Brangwyn to paint large murals, and this offer was taken up by the Vicar, the Reverend Arthur Swayne and by Frank Brangwyn.

After more than two years of studies and sketches, and getting towards completion of the murals, Brangwyn developed a fear that the air of Leeds would rapidly discolour them, and coat them with a layer of grease. His proposal to Kitson in 1913 that the painted panels should be scrapped and the work carried out in mosaic was accepted. Sylvester Sparrow and Henry Jesse Rust interpreted Frank Brangwyn's designs and reproduced their colours faithfully in the mosaics.

The St Aidan's Church Plaque was sponsored by Mr. Noel Squires, Landlord of the New Roscoe Inn and unveiled by him on 23rd April 1995. It is at St. Aidan's Church Roundhay Road, Leeds 8.

The attribution of the church to W S Hicks was a very rare and regretted error in the texts of our plaques.

THE VICTORIAN CENTRE

In the eighteenth century Leeds was the marketing centre of the West Riding's woollen cloth industry. In the nineteenth century it became the manufacturing, commercial and retailing capital of Yorkshire. In addition to its 'thousand trades', it provided services of all kinds to its region. This role was reflected in its wholesale marketing and distribution services, such as its large corn exchange, its extensive warehousing. and its major transport facilities. People and firms from far and wide came to take advantage of its financial institutions, courts and legal services, medical and educational institutions and a host of other facilities.

The town's first bank, later to be known as Beckett's Bank, was established in 1758. By 1827 Leeds had four banks of considerable size and reputation. Wishing to promote the financial stability of banks in the region and recognising the town's importance, the Bank of England established a branch in Leeds in 1827. The town was subsequently to become the home to many more banks, insurance companies and had its own stock exchange.

Leeds has long claimed to be the shopping capital of the North. Anyone seeing the fine Victorian and Edwardian shops and market buildings which enrich the city today can have no doubt why. It was from the 1820s, in particular, that elegant purpose-built shops began to be erected. Today the shops built on Boar Lane in the 1860s are much to be admired but so too is the shop and office building on Cookridge Street designed by Cuthbert Brodrick in the same decade. When available street frontages could no longer meet the great demand for retail space, the opportunity offered by the Briggate yards was seized upon to the create the splendid arcades which are one of the great joys of Leeds.

THE ROYAL EXCHANGE OPENED IN 1875, CORNER OF PARK ROW AND BOAR LANE.

The town's role as a flourishing industrial, commercial and service centre meant that it had thousands of visitors. By the Victorian period the traditional coaching inns and small hotels could not cope with the volume of demand. The Victoria Hotel and the Hotel Metropole respectively are fine examples of the medium size family and commercial hotels of the period and the grand hotels of the railway age.

Bank of England

The Bank of England opened a Branch in Leeds in 1827. These premises entered from South Parade, were designed by Philip Hardwick and erected 1862 - 64. The Bank remained on this site until moving to King Street in 1971.

The origins of the Bank of England's presence in Leeds, which dates back over 170 years, can be traced back to the Bank's decision in the 1820s to establish a network of Branches in cities outside London in response to problems caused by the widespread failure of many local banknote-issuing banks in that period.

Between July 1826 and December 1829, the Bank opened eleven branches: in Birmingham, Bristol, Exeter, Gloucester, Hull, Leeds, Liverpool, Manchester, Newcastle, Norwich and Swansea. The Leeds Branch, which came seventh chronologically in that list, was opened on 23rd August 1827. It first occupied rented premises on Boar Lane, then in 1835 moved to 19 Albion Street. In 1861 it was decided to construct purpose-built premises, and the site fronting Park Row and South Parade was acquired. Philip C. Hardwick was commissioned to design the new building, which opened for business in 1865.

The Bank of England then remained in Hardwick's building for more than one hundred years, moving to the King Street building in 1971.

The King Street building was designed by the Building Design Partnership and built by the Leeds office of Shepherd Construction Ltd.

Over the last thirty years many changes have been made to the functions that the Bank of England undertakes outside London with, in particular, the progressive concentration of wholesale banknote distribution on a smaller number of centres, resulting in Branch closures. That process culminated, in mid 1997, in the closure of four of the then five remaining Branches (Birmingham, Bristol, Manchester and Newcastle). That left note distribution to be undertaken from just two locations - London and Leeds, where the re-titled Leeds Cash Centre continues to operate from the King Street building, and undertakes in modern form the principal role for which the Bank of England's South Parade Branch was built.

As the Branch network has been closed, the Bank has expanded its network of regional Agencies through which it maintains contact with businesses in order to obtain up-to-date information about local economic conditions. Leeds is also the location of the Bank's Yorkshire and Humberside Agency, and hence is now the only UK city outside London where the Bank undertakes both note issue and Agency functions.

The Bank of England Plaque was sponsored by the Bank of England and unveiled by Councillor Les Carter, Lord Mayor of Leeds, on 11th May 1990. It is at South Parade, Leeds 1.

LOOKING UP TOWARDS THE HEADROW. HARDWICK'S BANK OF ENGLAND BUILDING ON THE LEFT AND FORMER ST. ANNE'S CATHEDRAL ON GUILDFORD STREET.

Brodrick's Buildings

These fine shops and offices were designed by Cuthbert Brodrick (1822-1905) the architect of Leeds Town Hall, the Corn Exchange and the Mechanics' Institute. They were erected in 1864 and renovated by Trinity Services in 1988.

Cuthbert Brodrick was born in Kingston-upon-Hull on 1st December 1821, the sixth son of a well-to-do merchant and shipowner. When he was 15 years old he became an articled pupil of Henry Francis Lockwood, a Hull architect who favoured building in Classical style. After completing his articles with Lockwood, Brodrick was financed by his father on a grand tour, studying the buildings in the capitals and major cities of Europe.

On his return to Hull in 1845 Brodrick set up in his own practice.

BRODRICK'S BUILDING

These fine shops and offices were designed by Cuthbert Brodrick (1822-1905) the architect of Leeds Town Hall, the Corn Exchange and the Mechanics' Institute. They were renovated by Trinity Services in 1988.

ERECTED 1864

In 1852 he entered the competition for the design of Leeds Town Hall and was awarded the contract for this very prestigious building which was opened by Queen Victoria in September 1858.

During the construction of the Town Hall he opened an office in Leeds at 30 Park Row, and later moved to 17 East Parade, and finally to 2 Park Place.

In 1860 Brodrick won the competition for the Corn Exchange, which was opened in 1862, and that for the Mechanics' Institute (now the Civic Theatre) which was opened in 1865.

In 1864 he also designed the two shops and offices numbers 49 and 51 Cookridge Street, fashioned in an unconventional interpretation of the Gothic style. This contrasted with the oriental design that he used in 1866 for the Oriental Baths which formerly stood next door. This was faced with bands of red, blue and black brick with freestone dressings around the cusped windows. On top there was a central group of three small domes, a tall striped minaret and small domes on the end of the pavilions. The Oriental Baths building was remodelled in a more conventional Gothic design some twenty years later, and demolished in 1969. One of Brodrick's last great building projects was the Grand Hotel in Scarborough opened in 1867. In 1870 he took up residence in Paris, and effectively retired as an architect.

The Brodrick's Building Plaque was sponsored by Trinity Services (Developers) and unveiled by Mr. John M. Quinlan, Director, on 20th July, 1989. It is in Cookridge Street, Leeds 2.

Queen's Arcade

Named in honour of Queen Victoria's Golden Jubilee. Designed by Edward Clark and built in 1888-9 by Armistead & Proctor on the site of the Rose and Crown coaching inn which occupied one of Briggate's medieval burgage plots.

Briggate is famous for its fine Victorian and Edwardian arcades. When there was no longer any space on the town's main streets for new shops, the imaginative solution was found of building arcades on the sites of the medieval burgage plots laid out on both sides of Briggate in 1207. The first arcade to be built was Thornton's, opened in 1878. The second and one of its finest was the Queen's Arcade completed in 1889.

It was erected on the site of the Rose and Crown Yard, home of the Rose and Crown coaching inn from where coaches used to set off to York, Sheffield, Scarborough and Liverpool in the Georgian period.

To the absolute horror of Leeds people, it was at the Rose and Crown Yard in November 1831 that the police seized a mysterious package waiting to go on a coach to Edinburgh. It was found to contain the body of Robert Hudson - a victim of the Leeds bodysnatchers who had exhumed his body from the Parish Church graveyard and were sending it to an Edinburgh surgeon.

The arcade was built by Armistead and Proctor. William Armistead was a builders and hardware merchant who had a shop in Briggate a little below the Rose and Crown Yard. The designs were prepared by Edward Clark, a London architect. The arcade's principal entrance was from Lands Lane, and initially the Briggate entrance was via a narrow passageway alongside Foster's shop.

To draw attention to the Briggate entrance the large but plain Pott's clock, familiar to us today, was erected.

The more imposing Briggate frontage was created in 1895. When the arcade opened the *Yorkshire Post* noted 'The edifice is light, bright and architecturally elegant, and is, moreover, admirably designed from the business point of view.' The arcade is distinguished by its sinuously curved cast iron balcony. Some of the balcony frontages were used as shops but originally it gave access to the living accommodation of the shopkeepers.

The Queen's Arcade Plaque was sponsored by DTZ Debenham Thorpe and unveiled by Councillor Keith Wakefield, Chair of Leeds City Council's Development Service Group Committee, on 28th March 1999. It is at the Briggate end of Queen's Arcade, Leeds 1.

Victoria Quarter

Victoria Quarter was begun in 1900 with the opening of Frank Matcham's splendid County and Cross Arcades. Enhanced in 1990 by covering Queen Victoria Street, the site was formerly medieval yards, Georgian shambles and slaughterhouses.

In 1986 the County Arcade's owners, Prudential Assurance Company Limited, commissioned Derek Latham & Company, architects, to return the arcade to its past strength as a retail attraction. This commission was extended to include Cross Arcade and Queen Victoria Street. The project was completed in 1990. In addition to the skilful and sumptuous refurbishment of the buildings, the architects introduced the brilliant device of glazing over the 400 feet long and 75 feet high space of Queen Victoria Street. The new structure provides a dynamic contrast to the terracotta of the Victorian buildings and unites County Arcade, Cross Arcade and Queen Victoria Street as a 'Quarter' and turns the whole into a glass cathedral.

The spectacular stained-glass work by Brian Clarke follows the underside of the entire length of the new glazed roof over the street, flooding the space with rich colour.

The Victoria Quarter Plaque was sponsored by The Prudential Insurance Company, and unveiled by Councillor Keith Parker, Lord Mayor of Leeds, on 2nd May 2000. It is at the Victoria Quarter between Vicar Lane and Briggate, Leeds 1.

County Arcade was the last of the Victorian Arcades to be built in Leeds. With its extension, Cross Arcade, it was the largest and most sumptuous, and formed part of the major redevelopment of the area between Briggate and Vicar Lane carried out between 1897 and 1902 by the Leeds Estates Limited. The whole scheme, which included the Empire Theatre, was designed by Frank Matcham, the London architect who designed over one hundred theatres and music halls throughout the country, including the Coliseum and Paladium theatres in London.

Matcham used a combination of Burmantofts faience, rich marbles, gilded mosaics and handsome carved and polished mahogany in creating two streets, two arcades and the Empire Theatre. They must have provided a spectacular contrast to the previous insanitary condition of the site, which included butcher's shambles erected in 1826, a group of slaughterhouses and a labyrinth of yards dating from the Middle Ages.

The County Arcade fell into a somewhat shabby decline from the 1960s, the trend being hastened by the closing of the Empire Theatre in 1961 and its replacement by the ugly Empire Arcade.

The Victoria Hotel

The Victoria Hotel was built in 1865 to serve people attending the Assize Courts newly held at Leeds Town Hall. Its stylish accommodation then comprised spacious dining rooms and bars, a billiard room and large meeting room, private sitting rooms and 28 bedrooms.

The Victoria is one of the best loved and most interesting public houses in Leeds, particularly because of its splendid Victorian interior. For many years its situation opposite the back of the Town Hall made it a popular haunt for the legal profession, concert goers, and the general public. It was built in 1865 specifically to serve the business generated by the first assize courts held at Leeds Town Hall. Advertisements in the *Leeds Intelligencer* of 1865 reveal that Harrison's Victoria Hotel - as it was then known - offered 'First class accommodation for visitors, commodious rooms for arbitration committees etc, Hot and Cold Baths. Dinners daily from one to three o'clock - joints, vegetables, cheese, etc, 1s 6d; with soup or pastry, etc, 2s including attendance. Parties having business at the Assizes will meet with first-class sleeping and general accommodation'.

The holding of the Assizes in Leeds was a great public occasion. When Mr. Justice Mellor arrived in Leeds on 12th August 1865 to open the West Riding Assizes (just seven days after the Victoria opened) he was carried from the railway station to the Town Hall in procession in the State Coach. The following day another procession went from the Town Hall to the Parish Church for a special service to mark the start of the Assizes. A special concert was also held at the Town Hall.

At these Summer Sessions ninety prisoners were tried - two for murder. Mr. Justice Mellor heartily thanked the gentlemen of the area for their readiness to sit on the juries and their sense of public duty.

In 1874 the hotel and refreshment rooms were purchased by the Victoria Hotel Company. In 1888 is was noted that its wine and spirit bars were 'the most spacious and convenient in the district', its ground floor had a lofty and well-lighted restaurant, its first floor had billiard, commercial, coffee and dining rooms, and a butler's pantry, and its second and third floors were occupied by private sitting rooms and twenty-eight bedrooms. Today the Victoria is a pub rather than an hotel, and is now under the care and management of Bass plc.

The Victoria Hotel Plaque was sponsored by Joshua Tetley & Sons Ltd and unveiled by Mr. John Power MBE Deputy Lord Lieutenant of West Yorkshire, on 25th April 1989. It is in Great George Street, Leeds 1.

Hotel Metropole

This fine hotel designed by Chorley, Connon and Chorley is one of the best examples of terracotta work in Leeds. A remarkable feature is the large stone cupola taken from the town's fourth White Cloth Hall (erected in 1868) which formerly occupied this site. Opened 1899.

the building is planned a complete suite of rooms devoted to commercial men, divided from the rest of the hotel, ... On the first floor, in addition to bedrooms, are planned a large room for arbitrations or company meetings, a private billiard room, a ladies' retiring room, and several private sitting rooms. ... The lighting is by electricity.'

The pinkish-red brick and terracotta used in the building were made and supplied by J C Edwards of Ruabon (near Wrexham). This company was the largest manufacturer of terracotta in Britain. They had supplied Chorley & Connon with materials for the Liberal Club in Quebec Street, built in 1890.

The Metropole was located near to the railway stations and near to the business centre of Leeds, catering for commercial clients. Its luxuriously appointed public rooms continue to be used for exhibitions and for corporate and family celebrations.

The Hotel Metropole Plaque was sponsored by Crown Hotels and unveiled by Lord Strathclyde, Minister for Tourism, on 10th November 1989. It is at the Hotel Metropole, King Street, Leeds 1.

Hotel Metropole Limited was incorporated in 1896, and, with capital subscribed locally, built and owned the hotel. It remained essentially a Leeds Company until 1956 when the hotel was sold to Fredericks Hotels. It is currently owned by Principal Hotels of Harrogate.

The Hotel Metropole is one of the finest terracotta buildings in the city, being designed by Chorley, Connon and Chorley and opened in 1899 at a cost of £90,000. One of the most surprising features of the building is its large stone bell tower. The hotel occupies the site of the fourth White Cloth Hall which was erected in King Street in 1868. When this, the last of the Leeds cloth halls, was demolished to make way for the hotel, its fine stone bell tower was preserved and erected on top of the building.

The description of the hotel in *The Builder* magazine of 15th July 1899 noted: 'The grand staircase leads out of one end of the hall, other sides being occupied by the office, the hall porter's room, the passenger lift, and the doorways to various public rooms. The dining hall is capable of accommodating 250 guests. At one angle of

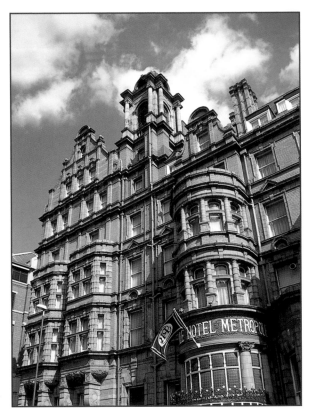

ENTERTAINMENT & LEISURE

For the wider community of Leeds the availability of facilities for recreation and entertainment on a large scale in the form of theatres, concert halls and parks was principally a development of the Victorian period and the twentieth century. During the eighteenth century and earlier, for the lower orders, leisure and entertainment was found at inns and alehouses, in street entertainers, travelling players, fairs, and gambling on the results of horse races and cock fights. For the better off most leisure pursuits were undertaken at home and, at least for the men, in the better class inns.

The two notable eighteenth century exceptions were the Assembly Rooms and the Theatre Royal. For much of the century the merchant families and better-off townspeople attended a variety of balls and social functions in the large room at the town's cloth hall in Kirkgate, the buildings later becoming known as the Assembly Rooms. In 1777 this was superseded by the splendid purpose-built assembly rooms above the newly built White Cloth Hall. Just a few years earlier in 1771 the town gained its first purpose-built theatre in Hunslet Lane, which attracted all classes of society provided they could pay the admission, though some thoroughly disapproved of such entertainment.

For much of the late Georgian and early Victorian period the Leeds middle classes lamented the lack of a large hall in the town which could be used for public meetings and above all public entertainment. In the eighteenth century concerts of classical and religious music were held from time to time in the Parish Church and in the Music Hall built in Albion Street in 1793. It was in 1858 when the Town Hall was opened that Leeds at last gained the grand concert hall that it had so long desired.

During the Victorian period in Leeds the era of the Music Hall became well established. The greatest of them all, built in 1865, the City Varieties Music Hall is still going strong. The later years of the century were also those of the creation of the great parks of Leeds. Golden Acre Park, one of the Council's more recent acquisitions, bought in 1945, is the first to be celebrated with a blue plaque.

Leeds has a great sporting tradition and many celebrated sporting occasions have taken place at Headingley, Elland Road and the city's golf courses. These are commemorated in plaques for Sir Leonard Hutton and at Moortown Golf Club.

The Assembly Rooms

Its handsomely decorated ballroom and card rooms made it one of Yorkshire's finest assembly rooms. Its patrons were the Leeds merchants and the local nobility and gentry. The ground floor formed the northern range of the third White Cloth Hall. Opened 9 June, 1777.

When the woollen merchants of Leeds decided to erect a new hall for the sale of undyed or white cloth in 1774, they took the opportunity to add another storey at its northern end to serve as a much needed new Assembly Rooms.

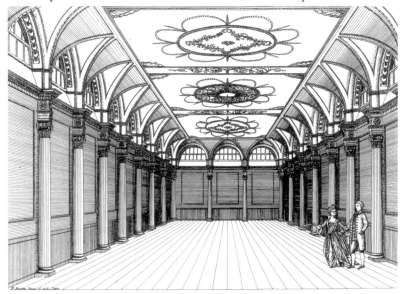

The Old Assembly Rooms in Kirkgate, built as the first White Cloth Hall, had become 'incommodius in point of situation as well as extent'. The new rooms, 205 feet by 33 feet, were completed by 1777. Tickets for the opening ball were half a guinea, and would admit one gentleman and two ladies. *The Leeds Intelligencer* described the opening: 'On Monday the ninth instant, the new Assembly Rooms in this town were opened, by the most brilliant appearance of genteel company, that were ever assembled together here, upon any occasion. The ball was opened by the Hon Sir George Savile Bart, and the Countess of Effingham, there were besides, upwards of two hundred gentlemen and ladies present, who all appeared to be competitors for politeness of behaviour gentility and complaisance. The company in general were very agreeably surprised at the neatness and elegance of the different apartments, which are allowed on all hands, to be as complete and highly finished as any set of rooms of that kind in the whole Kingdom.' A description of the ball given by the Yorkshire Archers on 26th October 1790 illustrates another splendid occasion: 'The company consisted of 200 ladies and gentlemen of the first rank and fashion in the county. The ladies appeared in white, with green ornaments, and afforded the greatest display in taste and elegance. The ball was opened at nine o'clock by a minuet danced by Earl Fitzwilliam and the Countess of Mexborough (patron & patroness of the society), the superior gracefulness of which was admired by the whole company. Country dances commenced at 10, and the supper room was opened at 12 o'clock. It would be impossible to describe the decorations of the table. Dancing continued till 3 o'clock in the morning, soon after which the company began to retire, highly gratified with their evening's amusement.'

By the 1860s the Assembly Rooms had lost the patronage of the local elite and become a Working Men's Institute, and was closed in 1866 when the North-Eastern Railway Company obtained the site of the White Cloth Hall as part of its scheme to build what is now Leeds City Station.

In 1922 the building was acquired by L. Hirst & Son, wholesale tobacconists, who fitted it out with beautiful polished mahogany fittings as their cigar, cigarette and fancy goods showrooms and tobacco warehouse. After occupying the building for almost seventy years, Hirsts sold it and it became the Waterloo Antiques Centre. Today, beautifully renovated, it has returned to its origins in the guise of two cafe-bars and a nightclub.

The Assembly Rooms Plaque was sponsored by the then owner of Waterloo Antiques, Mr. Bruce Bettison and unveiled by Mr. Bettison senior on 27th April 1989. It is on Crown Street, Leeds 2.

Leeds Town Hall

This greatest of monuments to Victorian municipal government was opened by Queen Victoria on 7 September 1858. Its architect, Cuthbert Brodrick, created a civic palace with courts, council chamber, mayor's parlour, offices, bridewell and concert hall, the whole crowned by a magnificent tower.

Dr. Heaton, a distinguished Leeds Doctor and proponent for the construction of the Town Hall in the early 1850s, urged: 'If a noble municipal palace that might fairly vie with some of the best Town Halls of the Continent were to be erected in the middle of their hitherto squalid and unbeautiful town, it would become a potential admonition to the populace of the value of beauty and art, and in course of time men would learn to live up to it.'

This must have expressed the popular opinion of the day. In June 1852 a competition for the design of the Town Hall was advertised. The committee advised by Sir Charles Barry, the architect responsible for the building of the Houses of Parliament, chose the designs of Cuthbert Brodrick then aged 29. (see page 64)

During 1854 and 1855 extensive modifications were made to the original design, and the tower was the subject of prolonged controversy. Some views were that as the tower would be non-functional, and purely for display, it would be a waste of rate-payers' money. Fortunately the Council decided to go ahead with the tower, and the clock and bell.

The Town Hall was opened by Queen Victoria on Tuesday 7th September 1858 with a tremendous celebration. The mills and factories were closed for the day, and enthusiastic crowds packed the lavishly decorated city from early morning to midnight. The statue of Queen Victoria in the main entrance marks this grand opening ceremony.

When it was constructed the Town Hall included the Law Courts and the West Riding Magistrates Court, with Council Chamber, municipal offices, a suite of entertaining rooms as well as the public hall with its grand organ. The basement contained the Police and Gaol establishments, with their kitchens and offices.

After the opening of the Civic Hall in 1933 many civic functions were transferred there, and following the building of the new Combined Courts Centre and the Magistrates Court (opened 1993) nearly all its former official functions have been moved. Today Leeds Town Hall is used mainly for social and entertainment purposes, and as the offices of Leeds Leisure Services.

The Leeds Town Hall Millenium Blue Plaque was sponsored by Professor N. R. Rowell, Vice President of Leeds Civic Trust, and unveiled by Councillor Bernard Atha OBE, Lord Mayor of Leeds, on 27th November 2000. It is inside the Calverley Street entrance of the Town Hall, Leeds 1.

City Varieties Music Hall

Harry Lauder, Charlie Chaplin and Houdini performed in this Music Hall built in 1865 for Charles Thornton on the site of the White Swan coaching inn. Famous venue of the "Good Old Days" first broadcast in 1953.

appearances by such great stars as Lily Langtry, George Formby, Vesta Tilley and Harry Houdini. Perhaps the most illustrious star to appear here in 1896, with his clog dancing routine, was Charlie Chaplin.

About 1902 Stansfield's Varieties was renamed the City Palace of Varieties - often abbreviated to the City Varieties. This small theatre survived all the changing fashions and trends in popular entertainment. In 1941 the City Palace of Varieties was bought by Harry Josephs and under his

In 1857 Charles Thornton became the licensee of the White Swan Inn, in the White Swan Yard at the top of Briggate. At that time music hall entertainment was very popular, and during the mid 1860s he rebuilt the White Swan as a music hall, the building which exists today, with a public house in its vaults. It was named 'The White Swan Varieties' and later as 'Thornton's New Music Hall and Fashionable Lounge'. In the 1870s Thornton built the nearby Thornton's Arcade and Thornton's Buildings. He sold the Music Hall in 1877, and it re-opened as Stansfield's Varieties. A typical performance in 1878 began with the overture at 7.00 p.m. and ended with God Save the Queen at 10.30 p.m. It contained character and comic songs, a horizontal bar performance, a hat throwing entertainment, a Lancashire sketch, and other 'exciting and mirth provoking items'. The price of a pint of ale, therefore, included a rollicking and boisterous floor show.

Competition from other Leeds theatres and music halls resulted in Stansfield's Varieties being closed briefly in 1898, but it was re-opened in November 1898 by Fred Wood, the proprietor of the Scarbrough Hotel in Bishopgate Street, who already operated a popular singing room at his hotel. On opening night the bill was topped by the comedian Alec Hurley, who subsequently married Marie Lloyd.

Then followed a period of considerable success with

and his two sons Michael and Stanley's successful management it continued to attract good houses, and give opportunities to rising stars such as Max Bygraves and Frankie Vaughan. During Harry Joseph's management the BBC decided to televise Good Old Days from the City Varieties. This old time music hall, with the audience all dressed in Victorian costumes, was a very popular television show which ran for thirty years.

In 1987 the City Varieties was purchased by Leeds City Council.

The City Varieties Music Hall Plaque was sponsored by the Friends of the City Varieties and unveiled by Mr. Paul Daniels, magician and TV celebrity, who appeared many times at City Varieties, on 27th March 1997.

It is at The City Varieties, Swan Street, Leeds 1.

Golden Acre Park

Opened in 1932 as a large amusement park complete with a dance hall, ponies, a miniature railway, motor launches, a water-chute and a monorail. In 1938 the venture failed. The site was acquired by Leeds City Council in 1945

The opening of Golden Acre Amusement Park beside the Otley Road, close to the city boundary at the edge of Bramhope, on 24th March 1932 meant that people no longer had to set off on a trip to the coast or await the visit of a fair to enjoy a special day out. Motor launches, rowing boats, canoes, sailing dinghies and a 'drive yourself' motor boat circuit allowed visitors to enjoy the pleasures of the lake. A miniature railway nearly one and a half miles long circled the park, with the engines 'Robin Hood' and 'May Thompson' pulling the open carriages and a dining car. The list of attractions included tennis, pitch and putt golf, pony and donkey rides, a zoo, paddling pool, water chute, and a children's playground with its swings and roundabouts, helter skelter, exciting aeroflight monorail and mountain glide. These, together with the Galleon and other cafes, the Winter Garden, the largest dance hall in Yorkshire, and the Blue Lagoon outdoor swimming pool attracted many people to visit the park.

Unfortunately the park closed after the 1938 season. Immediately following its military use during the Second World War it was acquired by Leeds Corporation. It is now one of the major parks of Leeds, attracting many visitors to walk by the lake and through the landscaped gardens and park land.

Frank Temple Thompson (1897-1950) built Golden Acre Amusement Park. He was the son of Herbert Wright Thompson (1868-1928) a successful builder in Harehills, Beeston and Roundhay, and a pioneering local film producer, film distributor and cinema owner. Frank, who also developed interests in the movie industry, joined the family business after service in the Great War. In 1925 the Thompsons began to plan the Golden Acre estate, intending to build several hundred houses on the 300 acres of farm land they owned between Adel and Bramhope. However, the venture failed, and only a few houses were constructed on the site. In memory of his father, Frank erected a veterans shelter on Woodhouse Moor (now a takeaway). His last major project was the Parkway Hotel, erected in 1938 on a corner of the Golden Acre site.

The Golden Acre Park Plaque was sponsored by Professor N. R. Rowell, Vice President of Leeds Civic Trust, and unveiled by him on 25th August 1998. It is on the outside wall of the cafe in Golden Acre Park at Otley Road, Leeds 16.

Sir Leonard Hutton

Sir Leonard Hutton, Cricketer, (1916-1990) was born here. He played for Pudsey St Lawrence, Yorkshire and England, and holds the record of the highest individual score England v Australia, 364, at the Oval Cricket Ground, August 1938. Captain of England 1952-55.

Leonard Hutton was born at Fulneck in 1916. He is considered to have been one of England's finest batsmen. He made his first-class debut playing for Yorkshire at the age of 17 and within four years he was opening batsman for England.

In 1934 he made 196 in the county match against Worcester, the first of 129 centuries that he made for Yorkshire and England. In the test match against Australia at the Oval on 20th August 1938 he opened the innings and batted all through the first two days, and was out on the third day after batting for a total of 13 hours 17 minutes and compiling the record score of 364 runs.

A wartime accident resulted in Hutton's left arm being permanently foreshortened, and when he returned to cricket after the war he was forced to use a lighter-weight bat. Hutton remained a superb batsman and in June 1949 he scored a one month record of 1294 runs, including seven centuries. During his career in first class cricket he amassed 40,140 runs (average 55.51 per innings) and 129 centuries, including 6,971 runs (average 56.67 per innings) and 19 centuries in 79 test matches.

Hutton became the first professional cricketer to be officially appointed Captain of the England Cricket Team in 1952. He captained in test matches against Australia, New Zealand, India, Pakistan and West Indies. He retired from international cricket in 1956 and on 1st January of that year he received a knighthood. After retiring from Yorkshire in 1960 he remained active in cricket as a test selector (1975-77), columnist and fund-raiser.

The Sir Leonard Hutton Plaque was sponsored by Yorkshire County Cricket Club and unveiled by Sir Lawrence Byford, President of Yorkshire County Cricket Club on 14th October 1995. It is on the wall of the house 5 Fulneck, Pudsey, Leeds LS28 8NT.

Moortown Golf Club

Moortown Golf Club was the venue of the 1929 Ryder Cup match between the USA and Great Britain. This was the first occasion that the match was played on British soil. The home side was successful, winning 7 matches to 5.

Moortown golf club was founded in 1909, and its course was designed by Dr. Alistair MacKenzie. The opening was celebrated with an exhibition match between the Open Champion James Braid and the legendary Harry Vardon. The present clubhouse was opened in 1915. In 1929 the club was host to the first Ryder Cup match to be played on British soil.

Charles Scatchard wrote of this match in the *Yorkshire Post* 25th September 1993 'Motor cars were still rarities when, as a seventeen year old student, I set out in April 1929 to watch the first Ryder Cup match played in Britain - at Moortown, Leeds. Like thousands of others, I made my way by tram from Leeds city centre to Street Lane corner then walked the rest of the way to the course. Most of my fellow-travellers were, like me, forever smitten by golf after watching George Duncan's British team fight back to gain a thrilling 7 - 5 victory over Walter Hagen's Americans.'

'The Americans, uniformly dressed in navy blue pullovers, neat grey flannel plus-fours and two tone black and white shoes - in contrast to the British team's tweed suits of various vintages and colours - were a formidable bunch. They won two and halved one of the opening day's 36 hole foursomes, with Johnny Farrell (USA) producing a wonder shot at Moortown's final hole. Farrell, playing from among a cluster of marquees on what is now Moortown's car park, lofted a blind recovery shot over the club house roof to finish 6 feet from the pin to enable him and Jim Turnesa to halve their game against Archie Compston and Charlie Whitcombe.'

'On the second day in the first singles Duncan trounced Hagen - the Open Champion - by 10 and 8. Whitcombe beat Farrell 8 and 6, and Compston beat Gene Sarazen 6 and 4. The British drove home their advantage when the youngest member of the side, 22 year old Henry Cotton, overcame Al Watrous 4 and 3.'

Since then the club has hosted a succession of major amateur and professional tournaments for men and ladies and many of the world's leading golfers have competed at Moortown. A permanent record of these events is displayed in the club's dining room.

The Moortown Golf Club Plaque was sponsored by Moortown Golf Club and unveiled by Mr. Malcolm Tain, Club Captain, on 11th February 1999. There are two identical plaques at Moortown Golf Club, Harrogate Road, Leeds 17, one on the clubhouse and one at the entrance gates.

ART & CULTURE

The Arts have enriched the life of Leeds, even if before the twentieth century few people strongly associated with the city won national renown in these spheres. In the visual arts, talented architects and their sponsors have had a profound effect in creating the distinctive character of Leeds. Much of this work is celebrated by blue plaques. The fascination of ancient Egypt was brought to Leeds by the architect Joseph Bonomi and the Marshalls at Temple Mills. Thomas Shaw and William Bakewell were commissioned by Colonel Harding to bring the style of medieval Italy to Holbeck. In the Town Hall, Cuthbert Brodrick gave Leeds its most magnificent architectural symbol. Thomas Ambler brought the Moorish style to Park Square, while George Gilbert Scott and the Leemings designed buildings of great distinction for the Leeds General Infirmary and Kirkgate Market. Frank Matcham created the city's most sumptuous building in the County Arcade.

Until the late Victorian period, perhaps with the exception of J. M. Turner, the works of Leeds artists or artists working locally have been principally of local significance. Nevertheless, works such as the fine seventeenth and eighteenth century panoramas of the town by William Lodge, Francis Place and the Bucks, the late Georgian paintings of Leeds scenes by Joseph Rhodes and William Cope, the water-colours of Leeds streets by John Russell, RA, are of great value to us today.

LEEDS ART GALLERY AT ITS OPENING IN 1888

In the sphere of ceramics the output of the Leeds Pottery and Burmantofts Pottery brought designs of the most delicate and ravishing kind to a national and international audience. We know little of the men and women who created them but they were outstanding artists in their own right. In the spheres of music and theatre, Leeds has a splendid tradition, though performers or composers and dramatists of national renown were few before the twentieth century.

Six figures from the arts and are commemorated either by their own plaques or celebrated on others: William Congreve, the Restoration dramatist; Atkinson Grimshaw, the landscape painter; Arthur Ransome the author; the sculptors Henry Moore and Barbara Hepworth; and Frank Brangwyn noted for his wonderful mosaics at St Aidans.

Twentieth-century Leeds has spawned a number of celebrated and highly creative personalities in the Arts not yet the subject of plaques: Jacob Kramer, Peter O'Toole, Alan Bennett, Keith Waterhouse and Tony Harrison to name just five. The verdict of posterity will decide whether they and others will be commemorated in this way.

William Congreve

1670 - 1729

Restoration Dramatist was born here at Bardsey Grange on the 24th January 1670.

WILLIAM CONGREVE
1670-1729
Restoration Dramatist
was born here
at Bardsey Grange
24th January 1670

William Congreve shaped the English comedy of manners with his brilliant comic dialogue, his satirical portrayal of fashionable society, and his ironic scrutiny of the affectations of his age. His major plays are *The Old Bachelor* (1693), *The Double Dealer* (1693), *Love for Love* (1695), and *The Way of the World* (1700).

Congreve was baptised at Bardsey Parish Church on 10th February 1670. His father, an army officer, came from an old Staffordshire family. Like all army families the Congreves had to be mobile. The farmstead, Bardsey Grange, was part of the estate of Sir John Lewis, uncle of Congreve's mother. He allowed the young Congreves to make their home there for a couple of years. By 1672 they had moved to London, and in 1674 to Carrickfergus in Ireland.

William went to school at Kilkenny, the Eton of Ireland, and in 1686 he entered Trinity College, Dublin. He studied under St. George Ashe, who also tutored Congreve's lifelong friend Jonathan Swift. In 1688 the family moved to Stretton in Staffordshire, and in 1691 he was entered as a law student at the Middle Temple.

He was never a serious student of law, and in 1692 Congreve published *Incognita*: or, *Love and Duty reconciled* under the pseudonym Cleophil. He quickly became known amongst men of letters, and became a protege of John Dryden. In March 1693 he leapt to fame with the production at the Theatre Royal, Drury Lane, of *The Old Bachelor*. This was followed late in that year with *The Double Dealer*. *Love for Love* was the first play performed at the new theatre in Lincoln's

Inn Fields, and was again a great success. Congreve's most frequently revived play *The Way of the World* was produced in March 1700 at Lincoln's Inn Fields. This was his last play, although he collaborated in translating Moliere's *Monsieur de Pourceaugnac* in 1704 and wrote librettos for two operas. In 1705 he was associated with Sir John Vanbrugh, the playwright and architect, in the Queen's Theatre, writing an epilogue for the first production. He died in London on 19th January 1729 after a carriage accident, and was buried with great pomp at Westminster Abbey.

Congreve is remembered as the author of many well known quotations, including:

'Heav'n has no rage, like love to hatred turn'd,
Nor Hell a fury, like a woman scorn'd.'

'Music has charms to soothe a savage breast'

'Thus grief still treads upon the heels of pleasure:
Marry'd in haste, we may repent at leisure.'

'Music alone with sudden charms can bind
The wand'ring sense, and calm the troubled mind.'

The William Congreve Plaque was sponsored by Councillor David Hudson, who represents Wetherby District on Leeds City Council, and unveiled by Mrs. Bridget Ely (nee Congreve) and Councillor David Congreve, relatives of William Congreve, on 8th July 2000. It is at Bardsey Grange, Cornmill Lane, Bardsey, Leeds 17

Atkinson Grimshaw

Landscape painter lived here   1866 - 70

Atkinson Grimshaw was born in 1836 in a back-to-back house in Park Street in the centre of Leeds. While he was still young his family moved to Norfolk. David Grimshaw, his father having left the police force, became a driver for Pickford's, the carriers. The Grimshaw family had returned to Leeds by 1848. David was now employed as a collector by the Great Northern Railway Company and Mrs. Grimshaw opened a grocer's shop on Camp Road. When Atkinson left school he was employed as a clerk by the North-Eastern Railway Company. His artistic inclinations were sternly repressed at home, his mother threw his paints on the fire, and he had no opportunity for special training as an artist.

It must be assumed that Atkinson Grimshaw began his painting career by studying the works of art in the Leeds public and commercial galleries. He was influenced by the Leeds Pre-Raphaelite painter James William Inchbold whose father was proprietor of the *Leeds Intelligencer*, forerunner of the *Yorkshire Post*. He was strongly influenced by John Ruskin, whose book *The Elements of Drawing* was published in 1857. Ruskin insisted on a close study of nature.

Atkinson Grimshaw made many such studies, making frequent visits to Hyde Park, Woodhouse Moor, Adel Woods and Woodhouse Ridge.

In 1858 Grimshaw married Frances Theodosia Hubbarde, who fully supported his aspirations to become an artist, and in 1861 he was able to leave his job and become a professional painter. In 1866 they moved from Wallace Street, New Wortley to a new semi-detached house, 2 The Villas, Cliff Road, Headingley (now 56 Cliff Road).

During this period his work included fine landscapes of Yorkshire and the Lake District. His reputation grew, and in 1868 his paintings were included in a major exhibition of national art at the newly-built Leeds Infirmary.

Grimshaw's success led to major changes in style, and the production of a body of work which amply justified his early aspirations. In 1870 he moved from Cliff Road to the seventeenth century Knostrop Old Hall. At the height of his success he also had a studio in London, and rented 'Castle by the Sea' in Scarborough.

In his last years he returned to Headingley, taking a house on Ash Road - a short walk from Woodhouse Ridge.

FRANCES AND ATKINSON GRIMSHAW MOVED INTO NO. 56, CLIFF ROAD, HEADINGLEY IN 1866.

Some of his paintings are in the Leeds City Art Galleries, including: Tree Shadows on the Park Wall, Roundhay Park, Leeds; In Peril; Nightfall on the Thames and Leeds Bridge.

The Atkinson Grimshaw Plaque was sponsored by members of the Grimshaw family and the North Hyde Park Neighbourhood Association. It was unveiled by Dr. Tony Moyes at the request of Mrs. Sandra Wood, great granddaughter of Atkinson Grimshaw and author of 'Knight's Errand', a biography of Atkinson Grimshaw, on 18th July 1991. It is at 56 Cliff Road, Hyde Park, Leeds 6.

Arthur Ransome

Author of Swallows and Amazons was born here on 18th January 1884

Arthur Ransome was born near Woodhouse Lane, Leeds on 18th January 1884, the eldest child of Cyril and Edith Ransome. His father was Professor of History at the Yorkshire College, later to become Leeds University.

After attending school in Leeds he went to boarding school at Rugby before studying science at the Yorkshire College, but his preference was for literature. He first earned recognition as a war correspondent of the *Daily News* and by his reporting of the 1917 Revolution in Russia. He knew many of the Revolutionary leaders and played chess with them. Arthur Ransome married his second wife, Evgenia Shelapina in 1924. She had once been Leon Trotsky's secretary.

They returned to England in 1925 to live at Low Ludderburn in the Winster Valley, Cumbria, where he started writing *Swallows and Amazons* in 1929. In this house he also wrote *Swallowdale* (1931), *Winter Holiday* (1933), *Coot Club* (1936), and most of *Pigeon Post*.

The pleasant traditional village inn, the Red Lion at Lowick was a favourite with the young Arthur Ransome and his friends, the poets Edward Thomas, Gordon Bottomley and Lascelles Abercrombie around 1906. He liked the village, and after the Second World War he and his wife decided to make it their home. They purchased Lowick Hall and again used to visit the Red Lion for good companionship. It was at Lowick Hall that he wrote much of his autobiography.

The Arthur Ransome Society, founded in June 1990, is based at the Abbott Hall, Kendal, Cumbria. It aims to celebrate the life, promote the works and diffuse the ideas of Arthur Ransome. It seeks to encourage children to engage in adventurous pursuits, educate the public about Ransome and his work, sponsor research and be a means of communication for those interested in Ransome's life and works.

The Arthur Ransome Club of Japan contributed generously to the restoration of the sailing dinghy 'Mavis', the model for the 'Amazon' in Ransome's books. This boat is on display at the Windermere Steamboat Museum. His chess set, desk, favourite books and other items can be seen in the special room at the Abbott Hall Museum in Kendal.

The Arthur Ransome Plaque was sponsored by the Arthur Ransome Society and unveiled by Mr. Norman Willis, General Secretary of the Trades Union Congress, and a long standing member of the Arthur Ransome Society, on 2nd March 1993. It is at 6 Ash Grove, Leeds 6.

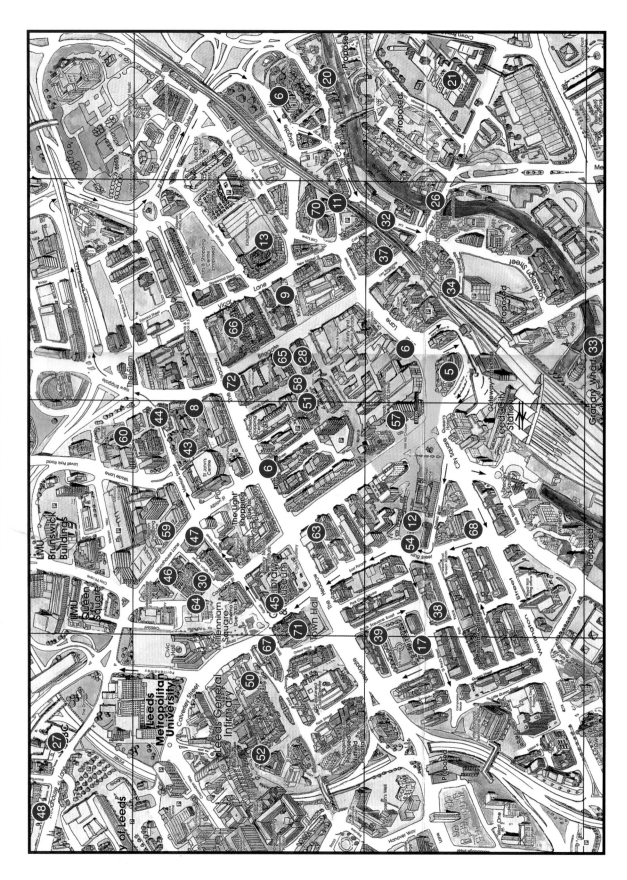

LEEDS CENTRE MAP